Understanding IAS 14

Segment reporting

Part of the IFRS in the UK series

Understanding IAS 14

Segment reporting

By PricewaterhouseCoopers LLP's UK Accounting Technical department
London, September 2003

Published by

145 London Road
Kingston upon Thames
Surrey
KT2 6SR
Tel: +44(0) 870 241 5719
Fax: +44(0) 870 247 1184
E-mail: info@cch.co.uk
Website: www.cch.co.uk

This book has been prepared for general guidance only and does not constitute professional advice. You should not act upon the information contained in this book without obtaining specific professional advice. Accordingly, to the extent permitted by law, PricewaterhouseCoopers LLP (and its members, employees and agents) and publisher accept no liability, and disclaim all responsibility, for the consequences of you or anyone else acting, or refraining from acting, in reliance on the information contained in this document or for any decision based on it, or for any consequential, special or similar damages even if advised of the possibility of such damages.

Appendix 1 is reproduced with the permission of the International Accounting Standards Board (IASB).

PricewaterhouseCoopers LLP is authorised by the Institute of Chartered Accountants in England and Wales to carry on investment business.

ISBN 1-84140-409-8

Typeset by Kerrypress Ltd, Luton
Printed and bound in Great Britain by Hendy Banks Colour Print

Contents

Chapter 1

Executive summary

1.1   Entities whose equity or debt securities are publicly traded, and entities in the process of issuing securities in the public markets, have to report financial information by segment in accordance with the rules in IAS 14, 'Segment reporting'. These disclosure requirements also apply to entities that disclose segment information voluntarily in financial statements where they are drawn up to comply with IFRS.

1.2   IAS 14 distinguishes two reporting formats: business segments and geographical segments. Entities have to provide segment information about both of these types of segments; more information is required to be disclosed for the segment format that is considered to be the 'primary reporting format'.

1.3   The way in which an entity is organised and managed and its system of internal financial reporting to the board and the chief executive normally reflects the dominant source of and nature of the entity's risks and returns (business or geographical) and, therefore, determines whether business segments or geographic segments should be the 'primary reporting format'. The other basis of segmentation becomes the 'secondary reporting format'.

1.4   If, however, the organisational structure and the system of internal reporting is based on both business and geographical segments, rather than being predominately one or the other, the entity should use business segments as its primary reporting format.

1.5   The organisational structure and the system of internal financial reporting to the board and the chief executive may not be based on either business or geographical criteria (for example, if it is by legal entity). In that case, the management should determine whether the entity's risks and returns are related more to its products and services or to the geographical areas in which it operates. In the light of that determination management should then choose either business segments or geographical segments as the primary reporting format, with the other as its secondary reporting format.

1.6   A segment is a reportable segment if a majority of its revenue is from external customers and:

■   its revenue (internal and external) is ten per cent or more of the total revenue (internal and external) of all segments; or

■   its result (profit or loss) is ten per cent or more of the combined result of all segments in profit or all segments in loss, whichever is the greater; or

■   its assets are ten per cent or more of the total assets of all segments.

1.7   If a segment is not a reportable segment because a majority of its sales are internal, but it still has external revenue that is ten per cent or more of the entity's total external revenue, that fact should be stated and the amount of the segment's revenue from external and internal sales should each be disclosed.

1.8   The external revenue of reportable segments must represent at least 75 per cent of the consolidated revenue. If it does not then additional segments have to be identified as reportable segments, even if they do not meet the ten per cent tests above, until at least 75 per cent of total consolidated revenue is included in reportable segments.

1.9   Segment information should be prepared in conformity with the accounting policies adopted in the entity's financial statements. If additional segment information is disclosed on a basis other than the accounting policies adopted in the financial statements, the measurement basis should be clearly described.

1.10 The principal disclosures for an entity's primary segment reporting include (for each reportable segment):

- Segment revenue, distinguishing between sales to external customers and segment revenue from transactions with other segments.

- Segment result.

- Segment assets and segment liabilities.

- Cost of property, plant and equipment and intangible assets acquired during the period.

- Depreciation and amortisation for the period.

- Significant non-cash expenditure, other than depreciation and amortisation, included in segment expense.

- Exceptional (by size, nature or incidence) revenue and expense for the period (encouraged but not required).

- The entity's share of the net profit or loss of associates, joint ventures or other investments accounted for under the equity method, if substantially all of those associates' operations are within that reportable segment, and the amount of the related investment.

- A reconciliation between the information disclosed for reportable segments and the aggregate information in the consolidated or entity financial statements.

1.11 If the entity's primary format is business segments, its secondary segment reporting format will be geographical segments, for which different disclosures are required. Similarly, if the entity's primary format is geographical segments, its secondary segment reporting format will be business segments, for which different disclosures are required.

1.12 The basis of pricing of inter-segment transfers and any change therein also has to be disclosed. Any material changes in accounting policies adopted for segment reporting has to be disclosed and prior period segment information has to be restated.

Chapter 2

Introduction

2.1 For companies that operate in a variety of classes of business or in a number of different geographical locations, the availability of segmental information, setting out meaningful analyses of revenue and results, is essential for good management. Such information is essential if management is to be able to detect trends in performance and sales within its specific business and geographical regions. Armed with such information, management is better placed to devise strategies and focus actions towards countering adverse trends or exploiting opportunities in specific business lines or market places.

2.2 The form of segmental information that is of use in a business depends to a great extent on how the management of the business is organised. A business may be managed on a product or service basis, a geographical basis, or on a mixture of both. The management structure of the majority of international companies, however, includes both geographical and product structures. Therefore, segmental information by product or service and by geographical region is relevant to most companies.

2.3 The value of segmental information is not limited to its application as an internal management tool. It also has an important role in external reporting, since by providing segmental information in financial statements, the company's management can explain to investors and to the market in general many of the factors that contribute to the result for the year. These factors might be developments instigated by management, such as the expansion of products or markets, or events outside management's control, such as political disturbances abroad.

2.4 For financial statements that disclose segmental information to readers to have real value, a high level of consistency of approach across reporting entities is required. This is particularly important in terms of determining what constitutes a reportable segment. IAS 14, 'Segment reporting', sets out rules for determining reportable segments so that different companies apply similar principles in determining what should be reported. This should enable readers of financial statements to make better comparisons of performance and prospects across reporting entities.

Objective

2.5   The objective of IAS 14 is to establish principles for segmental reporting. Segmental reporting involves giving information on the different types of products and services that an entity provides (business segments) and on the different geographical areas in which it operates (geographical segments).

2.6   Such information is provided so that users may:

■   Better understand the entity's past performance.

■   Better assess the entity's risks and rewards.

■   Make more informed judgements about the entity as a whole.

2.7   Because many entities provide several different products or services or operate in several different geographical areas, it is difficult for a user to understand, from aggregated information alone, the specific risks and rewards attributable to individual areas of operation. Segmental information is, therefore, important because it enables the risks and rewards of specific business or geographical segments to be appreciated by the user of the financial statements. Clearly individual segments may differ from one another in terms of profitability, opportunities for growth, future prospects and risks.

Chapter 3

Scope

3.1   IAS 14 came into force in 1998 and applies to complete sets of published financial statements that comply with international financial reporting standards. [IAS 14 para 1].

3.2   More specifically, the standard applies to:

■   Entities whose equity or debt securities are publicly traded.

■   Entities that are in the process of issuing equity or debt securities in public securities markets.

■   Other entities, not publicly traded, that disclose segment information voluntarily in financial statements that comply with IAS. In other words if such an entity wishes to provide segment information, it must do so in accordance with IAS 14.

[IAS 14 paras 3, 5].

3.3   If a single financial report contains both consolidated financial statements of an entity whose securities are publicly traded and the separate financial statements of the parent or one or more subsidiaries, equity accounted associates or joint ventures, segment information need only be presented on the basis of the consolidated financial statements. [IAS 14 paras 6, 7]. However, in the UK separate full financial statements of associates and joint ventures are not normally included with a group's consolidated accounts.

3.4   If a subsidiary, associate or joint venture is itself an entity whose securities are publicly traded (or that otherwise falls within the scope of IAS 14), it should present segmental information in its own separate financial statements. [IAS 14 paras 6, 7].

Chapter 4

Types of segments

4.1   Consistent with the objective of IAS 14 to provide users with information on risks and returns facing the entity, the definition of segments is based on an analysis of the risks and returns attributable to different products and services or different geographical areas. A segment is, in effect, a grouping of parts of an entity's operations that have risks and returns that are similar, but which are different from those of other groupings or segments. Such groupings are either business related or related to geographical areas.

4.2   In IAS 14 a *business segment* is defined as a distinguishable component of an entity that provides products or services and that is subject to risks and returns that are different from those of other business segments. Factors that should be considered when determining whether products and services have similar risks and returns (and, therefore, should be included in the same business segment) are:

■   The nature of the products and services.

■   The nature of the production processes.

■   The type or class of customer for the products or services.

■   If applicable, the nature of the regulatory environment, for example banking, insurance or public utilities.

[IAS 14 para 9].

4.3   Table 1 explains how Wella distinguishes its three principal business segments.

Table 1 – Wella AG – Annual Report – 31 December 2002

[6] Notes to segmentation (extract)

Pursuant to the "management approach" set out in IAS 14 our reporting follows the Group's internal structure. Accordingly, business activities in the Wella Group are divided into three business divisions: The **Professional** segment comprises all activities connected to the professional business; the division's portfolio consists in particular of the Wella, Sebastian and Graham Webb brands as well as salon equipment. Our **Consumer** segment (formerly Retail) consists of all activities in the end-consumer business, with focus on the Wella brand. The **Cosmetics and Fragrances** segment comprises all cosmetics activities with prestige and bridge forming our core business here.

4.4   IAS 14 explains that a single business segment does not include products and services with significantly different risks and returns. Whilst within a business segment there may be dissimilarities in relation to one or more of the factors listed above, the products and services included in a business segment should be similar in respect of a majority of the factors. [IAS 14 para 11].

4.5   A *geographical segment* is defined in IAS 14 as a distinguishable component of an entity that provides products or services within a particular economic environment and that is subject to risks and returns that are different from those of components operating in other economic environments. Factors that should be considered in identifying geographical segments include:

■   Similarity of economic and political conditions.

■   Relationships between operations in different geographical areas.

■   Proximity of operations.

■   Special risks associated with operations in a particular area.

■   Exchange control restrictions.

■   The underlying currency risks.

[IAS 14 para 9].

4.6   IAS 14 explains that a geographical segment cannot include operations in two or more economic environments that have significantly different risks and returns. But a geographical segment may be a single country, a group of two or more countries or a region within a country. [IAS 14 para 12].

4.7   The risks and returns of an entity are influenced both by the location of its operations (where its products are produced or where its service delivery activities are based) and by the location of its markets (where products are sold or services are rendered). The definition allows geographical segments to be based on either:

■   the location of an entity's production or service facilities and other assets; or

■   the location of its markets and customers.

[IAS 14 para 13].

4.8   In determining whether an entity's dominant source of risks and returns results from the location of its assets (origin basis) or the location of its customers (destination basis) the entity should look to its organisational and internal reporting structure, as this will generally indicate how management perceives the nature of the entity's risks and returns. The entity's organisational structure and its system of internal reporting to the board of directors or the chief executive (CEO) will, therefore, normally provide evidence of whether its dominant source of geographical risks results from the location of its assets or the location of its customers. [IAS 14 para 14].

4.9 Identifying geographical segments will often require considerable judgement. Making judgements involves taking account of both the standard's objectives and the qualitative characteristics of financial statements set out in the Framework; that is relevance, reliability, comparability over time of segmental information and its usefulness in assessing the risks and returns of the entity as a whole. [IAS 14 para 15].

4.10 For example, if all the similarity tests set out above are met, businesses within a recognised trading area, such as the European Union, might be segmented into 'home country' and 'Other member states of the European Union'. A further category of 'Other countries in Europe' could then be added to arrive at an overall total for Europe.

4.11 Classifying geographical segments simply into the continents of the Americas, Australasia, Asia and Africa may be too broad to provide meaningful disclosures. Appropriate account should be taken of the different risks and returns from operating in different countries within those continents. Depending on the circumstances, one or more individual countries might reach the threshold criteria laid down in IAS 14 for separate disclosure (see para 6.10) and the other countries in that continent that did not individually meet the threshold might be aggregated.

4.12 An example of a description of geographical segments is Table 2 Dairy Farm International Holdings, which also shows Australia and New Zealand separately as discontinued operations.

Table 2 – Dairy Farm International Holdings Limited – Annual Report – 31 December 2002

2. SALES (extract)

The Group operates in two regions: North Asia and South Asia. North Asia comprises Hong Kong, Mainland China, Taiwan and South Korea. South Asia comprises Singapore, Malaysia, Indonesia and India.

4.13 A reportable segment is a business or geographical segment identified based on the definitions above, for which information is required to be disclosed by the standard. [IAS 14 para 9]. This is dealt with in paragraph 6.1 onwards.

Chapter 5

Identifying primary and secondary reporting formats

5.1   As explained in paragraph 4.8 and in the section 'Reportable segments' below, the business and geographical segments for external reporting purposes will be determined by the entity's internal organisational and management structure and its system of internal financial reporting to its board of directors and the CEO (the 'management approach').

5.2   However, there is a further decision required to determine the format for external reporting. This is the decision as to which form of segmental reporting, by business or geographical segment, is the entity's primary reporting format and which is its secondary reporting format. Different disclosue requirements apply for primary and secondary reporting formats and these are described from paragraph 9.1.

5.3   The decision depends on identifying the dominant source of an entity's risks and returns. Where the impact on risks and returns is determined predominately by differences in the entity's products and services, its primary format for reporting segmental information should be business segments. The presentation of geographical segment information, therefore, is on a less comprehensive level. On the other hand, if the impact on the entity's risks and returns is determined predominately by the fact that it operates in different countries or geographical areas, the primary format should be based on geographical segments. The information reported for groups of related products and services, business segment information, is then secondary. [IAS 14 para 26].

5.4   Normally, the basis for determining segments, that is, the entity's internal organisational and management structure and its system of internal financial reporting to the board of directors and the CEO, will also be the basis for determining the predominant source of risks and differing rates of return and thus for identifying the primary and secondary reporting formats. [IAS 14 para 27].

5.5   However, where an entity's risks and returns are strongly affected by both differences in its products and services and the geographical areas in which it operates, as evidenced by a 'matrix' approach to managing the entity and to reporting to the board and the CEO, it will be difficult to determine a predominant source of risks and returns. In such cases, the standard requires that an entity should use business segments as its primary reporting format and geographical segments as its secondary format. [IAS 14 para 27(a)].

5.6   This reflects the IASB's belief that business segment analysis will frequently be the primary format and, therefore, assists comparability with other entities.

5.7   If, unusually, an entity's internal organisational and management structure and its internal financial reporting system to the board and the CEO are not based on either products or services or on geography, the entity's management should determine whether the entity's risks and returns are impacted more by products and services or by geographical factors and then choose business segments or geographical segments as the entity's primary reporting format. [IAS 14 para 27(b)].

5.8   A 'matrix' presentation, that is, both business segments and geographical segments as primary segment reporting formats with full segment disclosures on both bases, will often provide useful information if an entity's risks and rewards are strongly affected by both differences in its products and services and differences in the geographical areas in which it operates. IAS 14 does not require a matrix presentation of this kind, but does not prohibit it. [IAS 14 para 29]. In practice it is rare for entities to be unable to determine whether the predominant source of risks and returns is business segment or geographical segment, but several companies nevertheless give matrix type disclosures for some of their segmental reporting. FLS Industries, for example discloses revenue by geographical and business segments in a matrix form (example not reproduced here).

5.9   In some cases, an entity may have only one business or one geographical segment, within the meaning of the definitions in IAS 14. The single business or geographical segment can still be treated as the primary segment format if the internal organisation and reporting are predominantly based on this segment rather than on the other type of segment (business or geographical as applicable). No additional disclosures are required for the single primary segment if all the relevant information is already disclosed elsewhere in the financial statements. However, the fact that the entity is operating in only one business or geographical segment should be disclosed.

5.10   An example of an entity operating in only one primary business segment is given in Table 3 below Anglogold.

Table 3 – Anglogold Limited – Annual Report – 31 December 2002

2 Segmental information (extract)

Based on risks and returns the directors consider that the primary reporting format is by business segment. The directors consider that there is only one business segment being mining, extraction and production of gold. Therefore the disclosures for the primary segment have already been given in these financial statements.

The secondary reporting format is by geographical analysis by origin and destination.

5.11   An example of an entity operating in only one geographical segment is given in Table 4, mobilcom. In this case the disclosures given for the business segments are the primary reporting format as the geographical segment is presumably considered to be the secondary reporting format.

Table 4 – mobilcom AG – Annual Report – 31 December 2002

F. Segment reporting (extract)
As the group has virtually only domestic activities, segment reporting is only required by business segment.

Chapter 6

Reportable segments

Determining reportable segments

6.1   IAS 14 requires that business and geographical segments should be those organisational units for which information is reported to the board and to the CEO for the purpose of evaluating the unit's past performance and for making decisions about future allocations of resources to the unit. [IAS 14 para 31].

6.2   This focus on the entity's organisational and management structure and the internal reporting to senior management may be termed a 'management approach'. The management approach is a way of reporting segmental information 'through the eyes of management', that is seeing the business as the chief decision maker sees it. A pure management approach might require the entity to report all the information that is reviewed by the CEO when making decisions on resource allocation and assessing performance. However, that might involve disclosing an excessive amount of data. Therefore, IAS 14 permits aggregation and has quantitative thresholds for determining reportable segments.

6.3   Where an entity's internal organisational and management structure is not based on business units or on geographical units, the standard requires that the directors should look instead to the factors set out in the definitions of business segment and geographical segment rather than to the entity's system of internal financial reporting. [IAS 14 para 32].

6.4   In doing so any segments reported internally to the board or the CEO that meet the definition of a business or geographical segment should be treated as such and should not be further segmented. For other segments that are reported internally to the board or the CEO, but which do not meet the definitions of a business or geographical segment, management should look to the next lower level of internal segmentation that reports information along product or service lines or geographical lines. If that lower level reporting of segments is such that the segments meet the definitions in the standard of business or geographical segments, then those lower level segments should be treated as reportable segments, subject to the criteria described below (see para 6.10). [IAS 14 para 32].

6.5   As an example, geographical segments might report information on revenue to the financial controller of an entity for consolidation purposes, but the controller might report the information on a worldwide basis to the board and the CEO. In that case the reporting to the board and the CEO would not meet the criteria for a geographical segment and so the management would have to look to the lower level of reporting to the financial controller, in order to determine geographical segments.

6.6   The standard contains specific guidance for determining which business or geographical segments should be reported. Such segments are reportable segments, which are defined as business segments or geographical segments identified based on the criteria set out in the standard, for which segment information is required to be disclosed by the standard. [IAS 14 para 9]. The rules for determining reportable segments are described in the following paragraphs.

6.7   Two or more internally reported business segments or geographical segments that are substantially similar may be combined as a single business segment or geographical segment. Two or more business or geographical segments are substantially similar only if:

■   They show similar long-term financial performance.

■   They are similar in all the factors in the appropriate definition of business segment (see para 4.2) or geographical segment (see para 4.5). [IAS 14 para 34].

6.8 Combining substantially similar segments may be necessary where the internal reporting system is based on numerous business lines or geographical lines – say more than ten. In that case it is best to limit the number of reportable segments for financial statement purposes. Table 5, from Bayer's 2001 financial statements, is an example of this.

Table 5 – Bayer AG – Annual Report – 31 December 2001

Notes on segment reporting (extract)

The Bayer Group is managed on the basis of business groups, which are aggregated into reportable segments according to economic characteristics, products, production processes, customer relationships and methods of distribution. There are currently 14 business groups, which are aggregated here into 7 reportable segments.

6.9 Another reason for combining business segments or geographical segments is when several internally reported segments individually do not meet any of the threshold criteria described below. Additionally, internally reported vertically integrated operations might be combined for external purposes in an appropriate manner. IAS 14 encourages, but does not require, the voluntary reporting of vertically integrated activities as separate segments (see para 6.18 below).

6.10 A business or geographical segment should be identified as a separate reportable segment if:

■ A majority of its revenue is earned from sales to external customers; *and*

  ■ its revenue from sales to external customers (external revenue) and from transactions with other segments (internal revenue) is ten per cent or more of the total revenue, external and internal, of all segments; *or*

  ■ its segment result, whether profit or loss, is ten per cent or more of the combined result of all segments in profit or the combined result of all segments in loss, whichever is the greater in absolute amount; *or*

■ its assets are ten per cent or more of the total assets of all segments.

[IAS 14 para 35].

This may be illustrated diagramatically as follows.

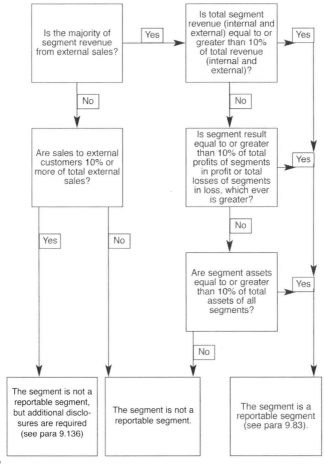

Example 1

Segment A has total revenues of 40, of which internal revenues are 25 and external revenues are 15. Total revenues, internal and external, of all segments are 350. Although segment A's internal and external revenues exceed 10% of the total revenues, internal and external, of all segments (the second condition above), it is not a reportable segment. This is because a majority of its revenue is not from external customers (the first condition above). This first criterion, that a majority of sales must be from external customers, has to be satisfied in all cases, before a segment becomes a reportable segment. That is, it is not an alternative to the other conditions, but is an overriding condition.

Example 2

Segment A derives a majority of its revenue from external customers. Its revenues, internal and external, are 40 and total internal and external revenues of all segments are 500. Segment A made losses of 10. The totals for all segments in loss (including segment A) and of all segments in profit were 90 and 200 respectively. Segment A's assets are less than ten per cent of the total assets of all segments.

In this case segment A is not a reportable segment. It fulfils the condition that the majority of its sales are from external customers, but to qualify as a reportable segment it also has to satisfy one of the other conditions. It does not satisfy the other revenue test as its revenue, internal and external, is less than ten per cent of the aggregate internal and external revenues of all segments. Nor does it satisfy the assets test. In relation to the profits test, although its losses are greater than ten per cent of the total of all segments in loss, they are less than ten per cent of the total of all segments in profit. Because the comparison required by the standard is with the total (profit or loss) that is greater in absolute terms, Segment A's loss of 10 must be compared with the total for all segments in profit, which is 200. As Segment A's result is less than ten per cent of the total of all segments on this basis, it does not meet the results test either and so segment A is not a reportable segment.

Example 3

Segment A has total revenue of 50, of which 40 is derived from sales to external customers and 10 is derived from transactions with other segments. Total revenues, internal and external, of all segments is 600. Segment A makes profits of 5 compared to profits of all segments of 60 (there are no loss making segments). Segment A has total assets of 200 and total assets of all segments (including segment A) are 400.

In this case segment A is a reportable segment. This is because it satisfies the overriding condition that the majority of its revenue is from sales to external customers and it also satisfies one of the remaining conditions, which in this case is the assets test, because its assets represent ten per cent or more of the total assets of all segments.

6.11 The standard's definition of segment assets is those operating assets that are employed by a segment in its operating activities that are directly attributable to the segment or can be allocated to the segment on a reasonable basis (see para 8.14 below). We believe that, consistent with comparison of revenues in the second bullet point above, which is clearly before eliminating inter-segment revenues, the basis for comparing total assets should also be before eliminating any inter-segment assets (such as inter-company trade debtors).

6.12 There may be an internally reported segment that does not meet any of the ten per cent threshold criteria. In such a case the entity may still designate it as a reportable segment. [IAS 14 para 36(a)]. One reason for such a decision might be that the segment comprises the traditional activities of the entity or that the medium-term expectations and plans are that this segment will, in due course, exceed the ten per cent criterion. Another reason might be that the performance of the segment depends more on market forces than all the other segments and is highly volatile. Lastly, the activity represented by the segment may be a new activity that incurs the entity wishes to highlight, such as a start-up activity that incurs costs, but does not yet generate much revenue. Examples of such activities in the past few years have been internet and digital television ventures.

6.13 If, alternatively, such a segment that does not meet the ten per cent criteria is not designated as a reportable segment, it may be combined into a separately reportable segment with one or more similar internally reported segments that are also below all the ten per cent thresholds. Two or more business or geographical segments are similar if they share a majority of the factors in the appropriate definition of business or geographical segment. [IAS 14 para 36(b)]. Note that for the purpose of combining segments in these circumstances, the segments need only be similar and not 'substantially similar'. In these circumstances, therefore, they need only share a majority of the factors in the definitions and not *all* the factors, which is a condition for combining *substantially similar* segments (see para 6.7). The distinction would appear to be that where a segment exceeds the ten per cent threshold, but is substantially similar to another segment it may be combined with that segment. If it is only *similar* it may not be combined. However, if a segment does not meet or exceed the ten per cent threshold, it may be combined with another segment that also fails to meet the threshold if it is similar to that other segment. It does not need to be *substantially similar.*

6.14 There is a third possibility for internally reported segments that do not meet the ten per cent thresholds. That is that they may be neither separately reported nor combined, but instead they are included as an unallocated reconciling item (see para 9.8 for the requirement to reconcile reportable segment disclosures with entity totals). [IAS 14 para 36(c)].

6.15 If, after determining reportable segments, the total external revenue attributable to those segments amounts to less than 75 per cent of the total consolidated or entity revenue (depending on whether consolidated or entity financial statements are being prepared), additional segments should be identified as reportable segments, even if they do not meet the ten per cent thresholds described above, until at least 75 per cent of the consolidated or entity revenue is included in reportable segments. [IAS 14 para 37]. Consolidated revenue for the purpose of this comparison would, by definition, mean external revenue as inter-segment revenue would be eliminated on consolidation.

Example

An entity has an internal organisational and management structure and a system of reporting to the board and to the CEO that covers three reportable segments.

However, the total external revenues generated by these three segments represent only 68% of the entity's total external revenues. The entity's systems also provide for reports to be made to the financial controller on five other activities that are together reported to the board as one segment. None of these five activities is individually large enough to constitute a reportable segment under IAS 14. The largest such activity accounts for 8% of total entity external revenue. In accordance with the requirement of the standard, the entity designates this activity as a reportable segment, making the total external revenues attributable to reportable segments 76% of total entity revenues.

6.16 Finally, a segment that is subject to internal reporting to the board and to the CEO may not qualify as a reportable segment, because the majority of its revenue may not be earned from sales to external customers. In such a case, specific disclosures about the segment may still be required if its sales to external customers are ten per cent or more of total entity external revenue, as described from paragraph 11.7.

6.17 The ten per cent thresholds in IAS 14 are not intended to be a guide for determining materiality for any aspect of financial reporting other than identifying reportable business and geographical segments.[IAS 14 para 38].

Vertically integrated operations

6.18 Vertically integrated operations are structures that combine many or all of the production and selling processes within one entity. An example is in the oil industry where the activities of exploration and production (upstream activities) and refining and marketing (downstream activities) are carried out within one entity. Despite this many international oil companies report their upstream and downstream activities as separate business segments, even though most or all of the upstream product (crude petroleum) is transferred internally to the entity's refining operations.

6.19 The standard's definition of reportable segment, which has the overriding condition that a majority of the segment's revenue is earned from sales to external customers, would clearly not require the upstream operations of such an entity to be reported as a separate reportable segment. However, the standard encourages voluntary reporting of vertically integrated activities as separate segments. Such reporting should include appropriate description including disclosure of the basis of pricing of inter-segment transfers. [IAS 14 paras 39, 40, 75].

6.20 An entity that treats vertically integrated operations as separate segments for internal reporting purposes may choose not to report them externally as separate business segments. In that case the standard requires that the selling segment (the upstream operation) should be combined with the buying segment (the downstream operation) in order to identify externally reportable segments, unless there is no reasonable basis for doing so. If there is no reasonable basis for doing so, the selling segment would be included as an unallocated reconciling item (see para 6.23 below). [IAS 14 para 41].

Prior years

6.21 If a segment is identified as a reportable segment in the current accounting period, because it meets the relevant ten per cent thresholds, comparatives should be restated to show the newly reportable segment as a separate segment, even if that segment did not meet the ten per cent threshold in the comparative period, unless restatement is impracticable. [IAS 14 para 43].

6.22 If a segment was a reportable segment in the prior period, because it met the relevant ten per cent thresholds, it should continue to be treated as a reportable segment in the current period even if it no longer meets any of the ten per cent thresholds, if management of the entity consider the segment to be of continuing significance. [IAS 14 para 42]. But in the next period, as the comparative would not qualify as a separate segment, this segment would no longer be reported in the current or the prior period, unless it qualified as a separate segment again in the current period.

Unreported segments

6.23   All segments that are neither separately reported nor combined and reported separately with one or more other segments (see para 6.13) should be included in the segmental reporting disclosure as an unallocated reconciliation item, that is as a segment comprising all other businesses or 'all other' category. [IAS 14 para 36(c)]. The business lines included in 'all other' businesses or as a reconciling item should be described appropriately. As explained above (in para 6.20) this also applies to internally reported vertically integrated activities that are not presented as separate business or geographical segments in the external segmental reporting disclosures.

Chapter 7

Accounting policies

7.1 Segment information should be prepared in conformity with the accounting policies used for preparing and presenting the entity's consolidated financial statements. [IAS 14 para 44]. Segment accounting policies are defined as the entity's policies for preparing and presenting the consolidated financial statements as well as those policies that relate specifically to segment reporting. [IAS 14 para 16].

7.2 Policies specific to segmental reporting include policies for identifying segments, methods of pricing inter-segment transfers and the basis for allocating revenues and expenses to segments. [IAS 14 para 25].

7.3 Whilst segmental information should comply with the entity's accounting policies as a whole, this does not mean that such group policies are to be applied to segments as if the segments were stand-alone entities. The standard gives an example of pension cost calculations that are made for the entity as a whole, applying group policies, but which may be allocated to segments, not by applying the group policy to the individual segments, but rather on the basis of salary and demographic data for the segments themselves. [IAS 14 para 45].

7.4 The standard permits disclosure of additional segment information prepared on a basis other than the group accounting policies. This is, however, subject to the condition that such additional information must be information that is reported internally to the board and the CEO for the purpose of making decisions about allocating resources to the segments and assessing their performance. The basis of measurement for this additional information must also be disclosed. [IAS 14 para 46].

7.5 An example of additional information given by several companies is to show orders and order backlog by segment (two examples - not reproduced here - are Ascom and ESEC in their 2002 financial statements), usually above the sales figures, computed in accordance with group policies.

7.6 Changes in accounting policies for segmental reporting that have a material effect on segmental information should be disclosed. Examples of such changes might include changes in identifying segments or changes in the basis of allocating revenues or expenses to segments. Whilst such changes will not change the entity's aggregate financial information, it will change the segmental information. Accordingly, prior period segmental information presented for comparative purposes should be restated, unless that is not practicable. The disclosure required includes:

■ Description of the nature of the change.

■ Reasons for the change.

■ The fact that comparative information has been restated or that it is impracticable to do so.

■ The financial effect of the change, if it is reasonably determinable.

[IAS 14 para 76].

7.7 An example of a company disclosing that prior year information has been adjusted to reflect new segments is Wienerberger in Table 6.

Table 6 – Wienerberger AG – Annual Report – 31 December 2001

Segment reporting: In accordance with the "management approach", the definition of business units for primary segment reporting should reflect the internal reporting structure. For regional segment reporting, sales are classified by customer headquarters. The new organisation of the Wienerberger Group led to a change in business units during the reporting period. Prior year data was adjusted to reflect the new segmentation.

7.8   If an entity changes the identification of its segments, but does not restate comparatives on the new basis, because it is impracticable to do so, it should report segmental information on both the old and the new bases of segmentation in the year in which it changes the identification of the segments. In other words, whilst it does not alter the comparatives, it gives additional information in the current year, being segmental information on the old basis as well as on the new basis. [IAS 14 para 76].

7.9   Changes in other accounting policies, that is, policies for matters other than segmental reporting, should be dealt with in accordance with IAS 8. The benchmark treatment under IAS 8, is to restate comparatives in accordance with the new policy. Alternatively under IAS 8, the cumulative adjustment may be included in determining the entity's net profit or loss for the current period, although in its improvements exposure draft, issued in May 2002, the IASB is proposing to eliminate this alternative treatment.

7.10   If the benchmark treatment is followed comparatives will be adjusted. If the currently allowed alternative is followed the cumulative adjustment is included in segment result if it is an operating item that can be attributed or reasonably allocated to a segment. In this case, IAS 8 requires separate disclosure if the size or incidence of the item is such that disclosure is relevant to assessing the entity's performance for the period. In addition, paragraph 59 of IAS 14 (see para 9.3) would encourage disclosure by individual segment. [IAS 14 paras 77, 78].

Chapter 8

Segment information

8.1   The disclosures required for reportable segments are considered from paragraph 9.1. The segment information to be disclosed includes the following items:

■   Segment revenue (see para 8.7).

■   Segment expenses (see para 8.8).

■   Segment result (see para 8.13).

■   Segment assets (see para 8.14).

■   Segment liabilities (see para 8.21).

The definitions and rules that apply to each of these disclosures are considered in the paragraphs that follow.

8.2   Segment revenue, segment expense, segment assets and segment liabilities are determined and disclosed before the elimination of intra-group balances and transactions except to the extent that such intra-group balances and transactions are between group entities within a single segment, when they are eliminated. [IAS 14 para 24]. Intra-group balances are then eliminated in the reconciliation of segment information to the reported totals of, for example, revenue and assets (see para 9.8 onwards).

8.3   The definitions in the sections below include amounts directly attributable to a segment and amounts that can be reasonably allocated to a segment. In determining which costs, revenue, assets and liabilities may reasonably be allocated to segments an entity should look first to its internal reporting system. The presumption is that the internal reporting system is most likely to have been designed so as fairly to reflect the costs, revenues, assets and liabilities of each segment. [IAS 14 para 17].

8.4   In some cases, however, an entity may have allocated costs, revenues, assets and liabilities to segments on an arbitrary basis or may not have allocated them. In the first case the standard makes clear that an arbitrary basis is not suitable for the purposes of IAS 14 and in the second it explains that where costs have not been allocated they should be allocated according to the rules in the standard, if that is possible. [IAS 14 para 18].

8.5   Paragraph 48 of IAS 14 adds some further guidance on allocation, stating that the way in which assets, liabilities, revenue and expenses are allocated will depend on factors such as the nature of those items, the activities conducted by the segment and the relative autonomy of the segment. It further states that it is not possible to specify a single basis of allocation that should be adopted. An arbitrary basis is, however not acceptable. [IAS 14 para 48].

8.6   Where revenue, expenses, assets or liabilities cannot be allocated on a reasonable basis, they form a reconciling item between the information presented segmentally and the entity totals for each of the items in the reconciliation required by the standard. [IAS 14 para 67]. An example of disclosure of basis of allocation including unallocated items was given by MobilCom in its 2001 financial statements and is shown in Table 7.

Table 7 – MobilCom AG –Annual Report – 31 December 2001

F. Segment reporting (extract)

Revenues of separate legal entities which do not completely relate to a single segment are allocated to segments based on connection time. Significant expense categories are allocated based on relevant criteria. Other operating income and expenses which cannot be directly allocated to segments are allocated based on revenues. One-time, non-operating expenses and income are not allocated to a segment.

Segment assets and segment liabilities are allocated according to the legal entity to which they belong.

Segment revenue

8.7 Segment revenue is revenue that is directly attributable to a segment, whether from sales to external customers or from transactions with other segments of the entity. Interest and dividend income, gains on sales of investments and gains on extinguishment of debt are excluded, unless the segment's operations are primarily of a financial nature. Share of revenue of a jointly controlled entity, accounted for by proportional consolidation under IAS 31 is included. Share of profits or losses of associates, joint ventures or other equity accounted investments is not included as this is not permitted to be included in consolidated revenue under IAS 28 or IAS 31. [IAS 14 para 16].

Segment expenses

8.8 Segment expenses are expenses that are directly attributable to a segment together with the relevant portion of other expenses relating to external and inter-segment sales that can reasonably be allocated to the segment. They do not include unallocated administrative, head office and other expenses, income tax or the share of losses of associates, joint ventures or other equity accounted investments. Interest, losses on sale of investments and on extinguishment of debt are also excluded, unless the segment's operations are primarily of a financial nature. Share of expenses of a jointly controlled entity, accounted for by proportional consolidation under IAS 31 is included. [IAS 14 para 16].

8.9 Allocation of costs and expenses to segments is an area of particular difficulty. IAS 14 gives little guidance on this and refers instead to other standards such as IAS 2, 'Inventories', and IAS 11, 'Construction contracts'. [IAS 14 para 22]. In practice these standards deal primarily with the issues of allocating specific expenses to inventories or construction contracts and do not deal in detail with allocating proportions of costs, although paragraph 12 of IAS 2 refers to allocating costs between two products on the basis of their relative sales values. A more useful example is given in example 8 of the appendix to IAS 36, 'Impairment of assets'. This example deals with the allocation of corporate assets between three cash generating units for the purpose of impairment testing.

8.10 In summary the corporate assets (headquarters) have a carrying value of 200, comprising the headquarters building at 150 and a research centre at 50. The research centre cannot be reasonably allocated, but an allocation is made of the remaining 150 between the three cash generating units, based on the carrying amounts of the three units weighted by reference to their remaining useful lives as follows:

Cash generating unit	A	B	C	Total
Carrying amount	100	150	200	450
Useful life	10 years	20 years	20 years	
Weighting based on useful life	1	2	2	
Carrying amount after weighting	100	300	400	800
Pro-rata allocation of the head-quarter building	12.5%	37.5%	50%	100%
	(100/800)	(300/800)	(400/800)	
Allocation of carrying amount of building	19	56	75	150

The research centre is not allocated, but is treated as a reconciling item.

8.11 An illustration of how the basis of allocation selected for common costs or assets can affect the segmental results is given in the following example.

Example

A company has three distinct business segments, A, B and C. Prior to the allocation of any common costs to these segments, the financial position of these segments is as follows:

	A £m	B £m	C £m
Net assets	2,000	300	800
Turnover	5,000	2,000	3,000
Profit before common costs	200	40	100

On the assumption that the common costs total £100m, the allocation of such costs on the basis of the turnover of each segment as a percentage of total turnover would lead to the following depiction of segment results:

	A £m	B £m	C £m
Profit before common costs	200	40	100
Allocation of common costs	50	20	30
Profit after common costs	150	20	70

This contrasts with the situation where common costs are allocated on the basis of the individual segment's proportion of total net assets. In this instance, the results would be as follows:

	A £m	B £m	C £m
Profit before common costs	200	40	100
Allocation of common costs	64	10	26
Profit after common costs	136	30	74

Thus, the basis of allocation chosen may have a material effect on the segment result that is reported. Despite this, the standard does not require disclosure of the basis of allocation, although voluntary disclosure is permissible.

8.12 In practice it may be possible to allocate some costs but not others. For instance, if a group bears the cost of managing properties centrally, it should be possible to allocate such costs reasonably fairly to each segment on a basis that takes account of the type, age and value of properties used by each segment. Similarly, central administrative overheads in respect of personnel might be allocated on the basis of the number of employees in each segment. If different bases are appropriate for different types of common costs it would be reasonable to apply the appropriate basis in allocating each of the types of cost.

Segment result

8.13 Segment result is segment revenue less segment expense, before adjustment for minority interests. [IAS 14 para 16].

Segment assets

8.14 Segment assets are operating assets that are used by the segment in its operating activities and that are directly attributable to the segment or can be allocated to it on a reasonable basis. Segment assets exclude income tax assets. Segment assets are reported after deducting related allowances (for example, grants) that have been deducted from the assets in the entity's balance sheet. Where the segment result includes dividend or interest income (for segments that are primarily of a financing nature) related receivables, loans, investments or other related assets are included in segment assets. [IAS 14 para 16].

8.15 IAS 14 states that equity accounted investments are included in segment assets only if the share of profit or loss from such investments is included in segment revenue. However, inclusion of the share of profits of equity accounted investments in consolidated revenue is not acceptable under IAS 28 or IAS 31 and, accordingly, equity accounted investments should not be included in segment assets. However, the entity's share of operating assets of a jointly controlled entity accounted for by proportional consolidation under IAS 31 should be included. [IAS 14 para 16].

8.16 Segment assets generally should include current assets that are used in the operating activities of the segment, such as operating cash, inventories and debtors. They also include property, plant and equipment, assets that are the subject of finance leases and intangibles. There should be a proper symmetry, that is if the depreciation or amortisation of an asset is included in segment expense, the related asset should be included in segment assets. A description of segment assets is given by Ascom in Table 8 below.

Table 8 – Ascom Holding Ltd – Annual Report – 31 December 2002

1.19 Segment reporting (extract)
The assets of the segments include property, plant and equipment, intangible assets, assets from finance leases, inventories and work in process, accounts receivable trade and other current assets. The liabilities comprise provisions, customer prepayments, accounts payable trade and other short-term liabilities.

8.17 Assets used for head office or general administrative purposes should not be included, although where such assets are employed on behalf of a particular segment an allocation should be made. For example, property assets of a group might be held in one property company, but they may be occupied and used by several operating divisions or segments. In such circumstances, the property and related assets would be allocated to the segments on a reasonable basis.

8.18 Where assets are shared by two or more segments, they should be allocated to the segments on a reasonable basis. Paragraph 47 of the standard repeats the 'symmetry' principle described above (see para 8.16) that assets used jointly by two or more segments should be allocated to segments, if and only if, their related revenues and expenses are also allocated to those segments. [IAS 14 para 47].

8.19 Segment assets include goodwill that is directly attributable to a segment or that can be allocated to a segment on a reasonable basis and segment expense includes the related amortisation of goodwill. [IAS 14 para 19].

8.20 Where assets have been fair valued as the result of an acquisition or revalued because the entity has a policy of revaluing fixed assets, the values attributed to segment assets are those fair values or revalued amounts. [IAS 14 para 21].

Segment liabilities

8.21 Segment liabilities are operating liabilities that result from the operating activities of the segment and that are either directly attributable to the segment or can be allocated to it on a reasonable basis. Income tax liabilities are excluded. The entity's share of operating liabilities of a jointly controlled entity accounted for by proportional consolidation under IAS 31 is included. [IAS 14 para 16].

8.22 Segment liabilities include pension and post-retirement obligations, trade creditors, accruals, payments in advance, warranty provisions and other liabilities relating to the provision of goods and services. Segment liabilities exclude borrowings, finance lease liabilities, other liabilities of a financing nature and taxation liabilities. [IAS 14 para 20]. A description of segment liabilities is given by Ascom in Table 8.

8.23 However, if the segment is primarily of a financing nature and interest expense is included in its segment result, the related interest-bearing liability is included in segment liabilities. [IAS 14 para 20]. An example of company allocating interest-bearing liabilities to a segment is mobilcom in Table 9.

Table 9 – mobilcom AG – Annual Report – 31 December 2002

F Segment reporting (extract)
The group mainly operates in the following segments during 2002:

- Mobile telecommunications: operating as a GSM service provider

- UMTS: activities as a future UMTS network operator

- Fixed network/internet: range of fixed-line speech and data services, together with related services

- Other – activities not included in the above segments

Segment assets consist primarily of intangible assets (including goodwill), tangible fixed assets, inventories, receivables, other assets and cash and cash equivalents. Receivables for taxes have been excluded. Investments in associates and joint ventures, valued using the equity method, have been shown separately in the segment information. Segment liabilities are primarily those relating to the operating activities and generally exclude liabilities for taxes and financial liabilities. An exception to this are third-party, interest-bearing liabilities used to finance the UMTS license and the UMTS network construction, which have been allocated to the UMTS segment.

8.24 IAS 7, 'Cash flow statements', gives guidance on whether bank overdrafts should be included as a component of cash or reported as borrowings. It states that in some countries bank overdrafts that are repayable on demand form an integral part of an entity's cash management. In such circumstances, bank overdrafts are included as a component of cash and cash equivalents. A characteristic of such banking arrangements is that the bank balance often fluctuates from being positive to overdrawn. [IAS 7 para 8]. If overdrafts are included in cash and cash equivalents, they may form part of the operating cash that is included in segment assets (see para 8.16 and Table 9 above). If they are not so included, they will be treated as borrowings and excluded from both segment assets and segment liabilities (see para 8.22 above).

Chapter 9

Primary reporting format disclosures

9.1 As noted in paragraph 4.7 the definition of geographical segment allows geographical segments to be based either on the location of an entity's production or service facilities and other assets or the location of its markets and customers. Therefore, an entity's primary reporting format may be one of three types:

- Business segments.

- Geographical segments based on location of assets (where the entity's products are produced or where its service delivery operations are based).

- Geographical segments based on location of customers (where its products are sold or services rendered).

9.2 The required disclosures for the primary reporting format, whether that is business or geographical segments, are considerably more extensive than those for the secondary reporting format. The disclosures required for the primary reporting format are as follows:

- *Segment revenue* for each reportable segment. Also, segment revenue from sales to external customers and segment revenue from transactions with other segments should be separately reported. [IAS 14 para 51]. Inter-segment revenues will have been eliminated while preparing the consolidated financial statements and those eliminations will need to be reversed for segment reporting purposes and will form part of the reconciliation between segment revenue and the group's total revenue (see para 9.8 onwards). The definition of segment revenue is discussed in paragraph 8.7 above.

■ *Segment result* for each reportable segment. [IAS 14 para 52]. Segment result is the difference between segment revenue and segment expense before any adjustment for minority interests. [IAS 14 para 16]. The definition of segment expense is discussed in paragraph 8.8 above. Entities are also encouraged to report other measures of segment profitability, if such measures can be determined without arbitrary allocations. An adequate description of the measure should be given and if the measure is prepared on a basis other than the accounting policies adopted for the consolidated or entity financial statements, as applicable, a clear description of the basis must be given. [IAS 14 para 53]. Examples of such additional disclosures might be EBITDA, gross margin on sales or profit after tax. Segment result does not include share of profits of equity accounted investments. Requirements in respect of such investments are described below.

■ *The total carrying amount of segment assets* for each reportable segment. [IAS 14 para 55]. The definition of segment assets is discussed in paragraph 8.14. Segment assets do not include equity accounted investments. Requirements in respect of such investments are described below.

■ *Segment liabilities* for each reportable segment. [IAS 14 para 56]. The definition of segment liabilities is discussed in paragraph 8.21.

■ *The total cost incurred in the period to acquire tangible and intangible assets that are expected to be used during more than one period* (that is, property, plant and equipment and intangible assets) for each reportable segment. [IAS 14 para 57]. The amount disclosed is the total incurred (that is, on the accruals basis), not just the amounts paid in cash and reported as capital additions in the cash flow statement. Table 15 below gives an example of disclosure that splits the expenditure between that attributable to additions through business combinations (referred to as 'Additions from acquisitions' in the Table) and other additions to fixed assets.

■　*The total amount, for each reportable segment, of significant non-cash expenses, other than depreciation and amortisation,* that are included in segment expense and, therefore, deducted in measuring segment result. [IAS 14 para 61]. (See also the comments in para 9.6 and the requirements of IAS 36 for disclosure of impairment charges that are described from paragraph 11.15 below). Ascom and Novartis disclose reorganisation costs (which may include for example provisions for restructuring) by business segment in their 2002 financial statements. Dyckerhoff discloses non-operating expenses and the non-cash element thereof by business segment in its 2002 financial statements. (These examples have not been reproduced here). Table 10 shows mobilcom's segmental analysis of provisions and bad debts.

Table 10 – mobilcom AG – Annual Report – 31 December 2002

F. Segment reporting (extract)

2002 €000	Fixed network/ Internet	Mobile telecomm- unications	UMTS	Other	Group
Significant expenditures not using cash (excluding depreciation of non- current assets)					
Additions to provisions and accrued liabilities	39,905	88,963	416,442	21,502	566,812
Bad debts written off and additions to allowances	22,935	56,839	29	1,001	80,804
	62,840	145,802	416,471	22,503	647,616

■　*The total amount of expense included in segment result for depreciation and amortisation of segment assets* for the period for each reportable segment. [IAS 14 para 58]. The standard does not require separate disclosure of depreciation and amortisation of property, plant and equipment and depreciation and amortisation of intangibles, but this is sometimes given. Companies that give the analysis include Novartis and Danisco in their 2002 financial statements (these examples are not reproduced in this chapter).

■ *The aggregate of the entity's share of the net profit or loss of associates, joint ventures or other equity accounted investments,* if substantially all of those associates' operations are within that single segment. If such disclosure is provided, *the aggregate carrying amount of those investments* should also be disclosed by reportable segment, that is the balance sheet figure should be analysed by segment as well as the income statement figure. [IAS 14 paras 64, 66].

Whilst the above requirement stipulates that an aggregate figure is disclosed, the standard states that each associate, joint venture or other equity accounted investment is assessed individually to determine whether or not its operations are substantially all within a particular segment. [IAS 14 para 65].

9.3 The standard also encourages, but does not require, disclosure of the nature and amount of any items of segment revenue and segment expense that are of such size, nature or incidence that their disclosure is relevant to explain the performance of each reportable segment for the period. [IAS 14 para 59]. These items would equate to 'exceptional items', a term more familiar to UK preparers and users. IAS 8 requires disclosure of such unusual items. It gives examples including: impairments of inventory and property, plant and equipment; provisions for restructuring; disposals of property, plant and equipment; discontinued operations; litigation settlements and reversals of provisions.

9.4 The disclosure encouraged by paragraph 59 of IAS 14 changes the level at which the significance of such items is evaluated for disclosure purposes from the entity to the segment level. For example, an item amounting to 10 might not be significant to the performance of the whole entity, if the entity makes profits of 500 and, therefore, the item might not be separately disclosed in the entity profit and loss account under IAS 8. If, however, the item occurs in a reportable segment, which has profits of 50, the item might well be deemed as sufficiently significant to the performance of that segment for disclosure under paragraph 59 of IAS 14, albeit as stated above disclosure is encouraged but not required by that paragraph. An example of segmental disclosure of an exceptional charge that is also significant to the entity is given in the financial statements of ESEC and shown in Table 11.

Table 11 – ESEC Holding S A – Annual Report – 31 December 2001
One-time charges in the consolidated financial statements
The one-time charges included in the 2001 consolidated income statement are presented separately as a means of increasing comparability. These one-time charges include restructuring costs as well as non-recurring expenses resulting from the decline in sales and ongoing cyclical weakness in demand.

in CHF 1,000	2001
Valuation adjustments/provisions	(44,911)
Current obligations	(4,470)
Losses on doubtful accounts	(1,330)
Restructuring costs	(12,895)
Total	**(63,606)**
Cost of materials	(23,301)
of which in segments being discontinued	*(5,823)*
Operating expenses	(40,305)
of which in segments being discontinued	*(5,842)*
Total	(63,606)
of which in segments being discontinued	*(11,665)*
Die Bonder	(20,235)
Wire Bonder	(28,039)
Micron	(3,234)
Factory Integration	(8,871)
Other	(2,794)
Costs at group level	(433)
Total	**(63,606)**

The current obligations are a result of the discontinuation of certain business activities.

9.5   IAS 7, 'Cash flow statements', encourages disclosure of the cash flows arising from the operating, investing and financing activities of each reported business and geographical segment. [IAS 7 para 50(d)]. It states that disclosure of segmental cash flows enables users to obtain a better understanding of the relationship between the cash flows of the business as a whole and those of its component parts and the availability and variability of segmental cash flows. [IAS 7 para 52].

9.6 Where such information is given voluntarily, IAS 14 permits entities not to make the disclosures noted in paragraph 9.2 in respect of (i) depreciation and amortisation and (ii) non-cash expenses other than depreciation and amortisation. [IAS 14 para 63]. FLS Industries gives this cash flow information (and also shows depreciation and amortisation).

Table 12 – FLS Industries A/S – Annual Report – 31 December 2002

1. Breakdown of the Group by core businesses in 2002 (extract)

DKKM	F.L.Smidth Group	FLS Building Materials	FLS miljø APC activity	Other comp- anies etc.	Core activities	Non- strategic activites	FLS Group
PROFIT AND LOSS ACCOUNT (extract)							
Earnings before interest, tax, depr./amort. (EBITDA)	**250**	**726**	**(46)**	**(147)**	**783**	**(466)**	**317**
EBITDA ratio	3.5%	18.5%	(9.4%)	n/a	6.9%	(9.3%)	1.9%
Depreciation	111	305	4	15	435	369	804
Amortisation	34	87	1	0	122	38	160
Earnings before interest and tax (EBIT)	**105**	**334**	**(51)**	**(162)**	**226**	**(873)**	**(647)**
CASH FLOWS							
Cash flows from operating activities	**234**	**539**	**27**	**134**	**934**	**(220)**	**714**
Acquisition and disposal of under- takings and activities	18	59	0	(101)	(24)	691	667
Additions of tangible fixed assets	(114)	(290)	(3)	(1)	(408)	(225)	(633)
Other investments	(11)	192	0	68	249	693	942
Cash flows from investing activities	**(107)**	**(39)**	**(3)**	**(34)**	**(183)**	**1,159**	**976**
Cash flows from operating and investing activities	**127**	**500**	**24**	**100**	**751**	**939**	**1,690**
Cash flows from financing activities	**(462)**	**(467)**	**(50)**	**64**	**(915)**	**(695)**	**(1,610)**
Change in cash funds	**(335)**	**33**	**(26)**	**164**	**(164)**	**244**	**80**

9.7 In addition to the disclosures encouraged by IAS 7 and supported by further encouragement in IAS 14, IAS 14 also encourages disclosure of significant non-cash revenues that are included in segment revenue and, therefore, added in measuring segment result. [IAS 14 para 62].

Reconciliation of figures

9.8   IAS 14 requires a reconciliation between the segment information reported for the primary reporting format and the aggregate amounts reported in the financial statements. [IAS 14 para 67].

9.9   Segment revenue should be reconciled to total entity revenue from external customers (including disclosure of the amount of entity revenues from external customers not included in any segment's revenue). [IAS 14 para 67]. This reconciliation would primarily require elimination of intra-group sales.

9.10   Segment result should be reconciled to a comparable measure of the entity's operating profit or loss as well as to the entity's net profit or loss (after minority interests). [IAS 14 para 67]. As a consequence, all income statement data between operating profit and net profit or loss (after minority interests) should strictly be shown as reconciling items within the reconciliation.

9.11   Segment assets and segment liabilities should be reconciled to total assets and liabilities of the entity. [IAS 14 para 67]. Examples of reconciling items would be assets used for general or head office purposes and liabilities such as borrowings. Also, segment assets do not include equity accounted investments (see para 8.15), but these are required to be allocated to segments (see the last bullet point in para 9.2) and so these will appear as a separate reconciling item.

9.12   Note that in Appendix B to IAS 14 the example in Schedule A correctly shows separately investment in equity method associates and unallocated corporate assets and liabilities in the reconciliation for the primary reporting format (business segments). However, in the secondary reporting format (geographical) the example incorrectly includes these items in the segmental analysis of the carrying amount of segment assets. The total segment assets (excluding equity accounted investments and unallocated items) of 108 in the primary reporting format should be the same in the secondary reporting format (which incorrectly totals 175 instead of 108).

9.13 An example of a business segment primary reporting format is Table 13, Nokia, and an example of a geographical primary reporting format is Table 14, Nestlé. These examples reconcile segmental assets and liabilities to the balance sheet figures. Note that the Nestlé example treats goodwill and goodwill amortisation as unallocated items. As noted in paragraph 8.19 goodwill and goodwill amortisation are included in segments where they are directly attributable to a segment or can be allocated to a segment or segments on a reasonable basis. [IAS 14 para 19]. The other examples, Nokia and MobilCom (see below) do allocate goodwill to segments.

9.14 An example of a reconciliation that reconciles the result before interest and tax to net result for the year is given in Table 15, MobilCom (note that inter-segment transfers are immaterial and, therefore, are not shown). Only 2001 figures have been reproduced in the extract below.

Table 13 – Nokia Corporation – Annual Report – 31 December 2001

2. Segment information

Nokia is organized on a worldwide basis into three primary business segments: Nokia Networks, Nokia Mobile Phones and Nokia Ventures Organization. Nokia's reportable segments are strategic business units that offer different products and services for which monthly financial information is provided to the Board.

Nokia Networks is a leading provider of mobile, fixed broadband and IP network infrastructure and related services. Nokia Networks aims to be a leader in IP mobility core, radio and broadband access for network providers and operators.

Nokia Mobile Phones develops, manufactures and supplies mobile phones and wireless data products, including a complete range of cellular phones for all major digital and analog standards worldwide.

Nokia Ventures Organization exists to create new businesses outside the natural development path of the company's core activities. The unit comprises venture capital activities, incubation, and a portfolio of new ventures, including two more mature businesses: Nokia Internet Communications and Nokia Home Communications.

Common Group Functions consists of common research and general Group functions.

	Nokia Networks	Nokia Mobile Phones	Nokia Ventures Organization	Common Group Functions	Total reportable segments	Eliminations	Group
2001, EURm							
Profit and Loss Information							
Net sales to external customers	7 521	23 107	563	-	31 191		31 191
Net sales to other segments	13	51	22	-	86	-86	-
Depreciation and amortization	511	642	115	162	1 430		1 430
Impairment and customer finance charges	925	-	307	80	1 312		1 312
Operating profit	-73	4 521	-855	-231	3 362		3 362
Share of results of associated companies	-	-	-	-12	-12		-12
Balance Sheet Information							
Capital expenditure [1]	288	377	23	353	1 041		1 041
Segment assets [2] of which:	5 469	6 087	260	1 104	12 920	968	13 888
Investments in associated companies	-	-	-	49	49		49
Unallocated assets [3]							8 539
Total assets [3]							22 427
Segment liabilities [4]	2 084	4 867	283	258	7 492	-132	7 360
Unallocated liabilities [5]							2 666
Total liabilities [5]							10 026
2000, EURm							
Profit and Loss Information							
Net sales to external customers	7 708	21 844	824	-	30 376		30 376
Net sales to other segments	6	43	30	-	79	-79	-
Depreciation and amortization	354	467	102	86	1 009		1 009
Operating profit	1 358	4 879	-387	-74	5 776		5 776
Share of results of associated companies	-	-	-	-16	-16		-16
Balance Sheet Information							
Capital expenditure [1]	304	902	38	336	1 580		1 580
Segment assets [2] of which:	5 076	7 108	709	1 577	14 470	-688	13 782
Investments in associated companies	-	-	-	61	61		61
Unallocated assets [3]							6 108
Total assets [3]							19 890

Segment liabilities [4]	1 936	4 602	256	686	7 480	-685	6 795
Unallocated liabilities [5]							2 110
Total liabilities [5]							8 905

[1] Including goodwill and capitalized development costs, capital expenditures amount to EUR 2 064 million in 2001 (EUR 2 990 million in 2000). The goodwill and capitalized development costs consist of EUR 801 million in 2001 (EUR 597 million in 2000) for Nokia Networks, EUR 59 million in 2001 (EUR 475 million in 2000) for Nokia Mobile Phones and EUR 163 million in 2001 (EUR 338 million in 2000) for Nokia Ventures Organization.

[2] Comprises intangible assets, property, plant and equipment, investments, inventories and accounts receivable as well as prepaid expenses and accrued income except those related to interest and taxes.

[3] Unallocated assets including prepaid expenses and accrued income related to taxes and deferred tax assets (EUR 1 106 million in 2001 and EUR 565 million in 2000).

[4] Comprises accounts payable, deferred income, accrued expenses and provisions except those related to interest and taxes.

[5] Unallocated liabilities including prepaid income and accrued expenses related to taxes and deferred tax liabilities (EUR 1 077 million in 2001 and EUR 339 million in 2000).

Table 14 – Nestlé S.A. – Annual Report – 31 December 2001

1. Segmental information

By management responsibility and geographic area

In millions of CHF	2001	2000	2001	2000
	Sales		**Results**	
Zone Europe	**26 742**	26 285	**2 783**	2 753
Zone Americas	**26 598**	25 524	**3 531**	3 503
Zone Asia, Oceania and Africa	**15 458**	15 710	**2 598**	2 673
Other activities [(a)]	**15 900**	13 903	**2 149**	2 015
	84 698	81 422	**11 061**	10 944
Unallocated items [(b)]			**(1 843)**	(1 758)
Trading profit			**9 218**	9 186

The analysis of sales by geographic area is stated by customer destination. Intersegment sales are not significant.

In millions of CHF	2001	2000	2001	2000
	Assets		**Liabilities**	
Zone Europe	**12 508**	12 913	**5 384**	5 279
Zone Americas	**10 991**	10 503	**3 675**	3 460
Zone Asia, Oceania and Africa	**6 895**	6 897	**2 453**	2 591
Other activities [(a)]	**8 749**	7 860	**3 216**	2 896
	39 143	38 173	**14 728**	14 226
Unallocated items [(c)]	**30 419**	10 635	**1 160**	386
Eliminations	**(1 119)**	(849)	**(1 119)**	(849)
	68 443	47 959	**14 769**	13 763

In millions of CHF	2001	2000	2001	2000
	Capital expenditure		Depreciation of property, plant and equipment	
Zone Europe	954	946	806	890
Zone Americas	747	766	695	767
Zone Asia, Oceania and Africa	626	550	438	481
Other activities [a]	1 169	949	558	519
	3 496	3 211	2 497	2 657
Unallocated items [d]	115	94	84	80
	3 611	3 305	2 581	2 737

[a] Mainly Pharmaceutical products and Water, managed on a worldwide basis.

[b] Mainly corporate expenses, research and development costs as well as amortisation of goodwill.

[c] Corporate and research and development assets/liabilities, including goodwill plus, in 2001, assets/liabilities of Ralston Purina.

[d] Corporate and research and development fixed assets.

Table 15 – MobilCom AG – Annual Report – 31 December 2001

F. Segment reporting (2001 figures only reproduced here)

As the group has virtually only domestic activities, segment reporting is only required by business segment.

	Fixed network TEURO	Mobile Telecomm- unications TEURO	Internet TEURO	UMTS TEURO	Other TEURO	Group TEURO
Third party sales	332,880	1,919,342	249,903	0	87,577	2,589,702
Segment result	-20,193	-62,453	-29,939	-52,304	-64,071	-228,960
(of which good- will amortisation)	(0)	(19,889)	(4,799)	(0)	(4,566)	(29,254)
Share of results of companies included using the equity method	-385	0	-321	0	-7,131	-7,837
Result before interest and taxes	**-20,578**	**-62,453**	**-30,260**	**-52,304**	**-71,202**	**-236,797**
Unallocated expenses/income						2,757
Group loss before interest and tax						-234,040
Financial expence, net						-17,172
Taxes on income						42,011
Group loss						-209,201
Minority interest						3,627
Net result						-205,574
Segment assets	266,036	511,132	114,633	9,331,597	171,799	10,395,197
Associated compa- nies and joint ven- tures	1,824	0	0	0	0	1,824
Unallocated assets						634,212
Group assets						11,031,233
Segment liabilities	160,404	197,781	9,267	6,228,305	37,099	6,632,856
Minority interest						22,689
Unallocated liabilities						606,723
Group liabilities						7,262,268

Capital expenditure	25,749	25,632	19,885	763,024	88,737	923,027
Additions from acquisitions	0	0	1,529	0	0	1,529
Group capital expenditure						924,556
Depreciation and amortisation	43,096	81,818	15,768	10,567	17,256	168,505
Of which impairment write-downs	(6,763)	(3,068)	(0)	(0)	(561)	(10,392)

Revenues increased in the fixed network segment, but this segment suffered a loss, amongst other things due to impairment write-downs of switches and allowances for routers.

Chapter 10

Secondary reporting format disclosures

10.1   As noted in paragraph 9.1 an entity's primary reporting format may be one of three types:

- Business segments.

- Geographical segments based on location of assets (where the entity's products are produced or where its service delivery operations are based).

- Geographical segments based on location of customers (where its products are sold or services rendered).

10.2   In addition to the disclosures required for each of these primary reporting formats, the standard requires fewer disclosures to be made for the secondary reporting format and these disclosures depend on the segment basis chosen as the primary reporting format.

Primary reporting format — business segments

10.3   If the entity's primary reporting format is business segments, the secondary reporting format disclosures are as follows:

- Segment revenue from external customers by geographical area, based on the geographical location of its customers, for each geographical segment whose revenue from sales to external customers is ten per cent or more of total entity revenue from sales to all external customers.

- Total carrying amount of segment assets by geographical location of assets, for each geographical segment whose segment assets are ten per cent or more of the total assets of all geographical segments.

■ Total cost incurred in the period to acquire segment assets that are expected to be used during more than one period (property, plant and equipment and intangible assets) by geographical location of assets, for each geographical segment whose segment assets are ten per cent or more of total assets of all geographical segments.

[IAS 14 para 69].

10.4 An example of secondary segmental reporting format disclosures on this basis is given in Table 16, Nokia.

Table 16 – Nokia Corporation – Annual Report – 31 December 2001

Net sales to external customers by geographic area	2001 EURm	2000 EURm
Finland	453	494
USA	5 614	5 312
China	3 418	3 065
Great Britain	2 808	2 828
Germany	2 003	2 579
Other	16 895	16 098
Total	31 191	30 376
Segment assets **by geographic area**	**2001** **EURm**	**2000** **EURm**
Finland	5 087	4 688
USA	2 279	2 774
China	1 668	2 030
Great Britain	519	654
Germany	611	909
Other	3 724	2 727
Total	13 888	13 782

Capital expenditures by market area	2001 EURm	2000 EURm
Finland	477	587
USA [1]	151	279
China	131	157
Great Britain	34	75
Germany	37	133
Other [1]	211	349
Total	1 041	1 580

[1] Including goodwill and capitalized development costs, capital expenditures amount to EUR 2 064 million in 2001 (EUR 2 990 million in 2000). The goodwill and capitalized development costs consist of EUR 582 million in USA in 2001 (EUR 567 million in 2000) and EUR 441 million in other areas in 2001 (EUR 843 million in 2000).

Primary reporting format — geographical segments

10.5   If the entity's primary reporting format is geographical segments based on location of assets or based on location of customers, the secondary reporting format disclosures are required for each business segment whose revenue from sales to external customers is ten per cent or more of total entity sales to external customers or whose segment assets are ten per cent or more of total assets of all business segments. The required disclosures are as follows:

■   Segment revenue from external customers.

■   Total carrying amount of segment assets.

■   Total cost incurred during the period to acquire segment assets that are expected to be used during more than one period (property, plant and equipment and intangible assets).

[IAS 14 para 70].

Example

An entity has three business segments.

	External sales	Assets
Segment A	30	200
Segment B	130	50
Segment C	200	500
Entity total	360	750

In this example although segment A's external sales are less than 10% of the entity total, its assets are more than 10% of the entity total. Therefore, secondary segmental information must be given for segment A. Similarly, although segment B's assets are less than 10% of total entity assets, its revenue from external customers is over 10% of total entity external sales and secondary segmental information must also be given for segment B. Segment C exceeds both 10% thresholds and so secondary format disclosures must also be given for that segment.

10.6 If the entity's primary reporting format is geographical segments based on location of assets and the location of the entity's customers differs from the location of the entity's assets, the entity should also report revenue from sales to external customers for each customer-based geographical segment whose revenue from sales to external customers is ten per cent or more of total entity revenue from sales to external customers. [IAS 14 para 71].

Example

An entity's primary reporting format is geographical segments based on location of assets. It has reported as part of its primary reporting format sales on the origin basis (that is, based on the area where the products are produced or the service delivery operations are located) as follows:

	External sales
UK	240
Western Europe	400
USA	260
Total entity	900

Under the requirement in paragraph 71 of IAS 14, however, it must also analyse the external sales by destination (that is, based on where the products are sold or services rendered). When it does this the analysis is as follows:

	External sales
Asia	50
UK	300
Eastern Europe	100
Western Europe	200
USA	200
Africa	50
Total entity	900

The information that it is required to give under paragraph 71 of IAS 14 is, therefore:

	External sales
UK	300
Eastern Europe	100
Western Europe	200
USA	200
Other	100
Total entity	900

Neither Asia nor Africa represents individually 10% or more of total entity sales to external customers and so they may be combined as an item 'other' to reconcile to the total entity external sales. Eastern Europe, however, must be identified as a separate segment as its external sales are 10% or more of total entity external sales.

10.7 Similarly, if the entity's primary reporting format is geographical segments based on location of customers and the entity's assets are located in different geographical areas from its customers, the entity should also report the following segmental information for each asset-based geographical segment whose revenue from sales to external customers *or* whose segment assets are ten per cent or more of the related consolidated or total entity amounts:

■ The total carrying amount of segment assets by geographical location of the assets.

■ The total cost incurred in the period to acquire segment assets that are expected to be used during more than one period (property, plant and equipment and intangible assets) by location of assets.

[IAS 14 para 72].

Chapter 11

Other disclosures

Inter-segment transfers

11.1 In measuring and reporting segment revenue from transactions with other segments inter-segment transfers should be measured on the entity's actual basis for inter-segment pricing. The basis of pricing inter-segment transfers and any change therein should be disclosed in the financial statements. [IAS 14 para 75]. An example of disclosure is given in Wella's 2001 financial statements as shown in Table 17.

Table 17 – Wella AG – Annual report – 31 December 2001

[6] Segment information (extract)

Inter-segment sales are settled at market prices and are generally based on the same prices as those charged to third parties ("arm's length" principle).

11.2 If an entity changes the method that it uses to price inter-segment transfers, that is not a change of accounting policy and, therefore, comparatives should not be restated. However, as mentioned above details of the change should be given. [IAS 14 para 80].

Composition of business and geographical segments

11.3 An entity should describe the types of products and services included in each reported business segment and describe the composition of each reported geographical segment, both primary and secondary, if not disclosed elsewhere in the report and financial statements. [IAS 14 para 81].

11.4   The purpose of this requirement is to enable a reader to assess the impact of matters such as shifts in demand, changes in the prices of inputs or other production factors and the development of alternative processes on a business segment. Identifying the type of products and services included in reported business segments will assist in this.

11.5   Similarly, identifying the composition of geographical segments assists a reader in assessing the impact of changes in the economic and political environment on the risks and returns of that geographical segment.

11.6   An example of disclosure of the composition of business segments is given in Table 1, Wella. An example of disclosure of the composition of geographical segments is given in Table 2, Dairy Farm International Holdings.

Segments not qualifying as reportable segments

11.7   A segment may be subject to internal reporting to the board of directors and the CEO but, as mentioned above in paragraph 6.10, the overriding criterion for a segment to qualify as a reportable segment is that a majority of its revenue is earned from sales to external customers. [IAS 14 para 35].

11.8   Where the majority of the segment's sales are generated internally, the segment is not a reportable segment, but where its sales to external customers are ten per cent or more of total entity external revenue, the entity should disclose that fact. It should also disclose the amounts of revenue attributable to that segment from:

■   Sales to external customers.

■   Internal sales to other segments.

[IAS 14 para 74].

Example

Total entity sales to external customers are 100. Segment A has sales of 50 of which 40 are to other segments. Accordingly, it does not qualify as a reportable segment, because a majority of its sales are not to external customers. However, its external sales of 10 are 10% of total external sales of the entity. Therefore, the entity should disclose that segment A is not a reportable segment, because it earns a majority of its revenue from sales to other segments. The entity should also disclose that segment A's revenue from external sales is 10 and its revenue from sales to other segments is 40.

Previously reported segments

11.9 Previously reported segments that no longer satisfy the quantitative thresholds are not reported separately (but see para 6.22). Reasons why such segments may no longer qualify as reportable segments include declining demand, changes in management strategy, the sale of a segment or its merger with another segment. It may be useful to explain why a previously reported segment is no longer reported as this can help to confirm expectations regarding declining markets or management strategies. [IAS 14 para 83]. An example of such disclosure is given in Table 18, Odeon.

Table 18 – Odeon – Annual report – 31 December 2001

43 Segment Reporting (extract)

Primary reporting format by business segments

Internet activities as shown the previous year are no longer a business segment pursuant to IAS 14 (see no.44).

44 Discontinuation of Business Areas (extract)
As a result of a resolution of the Management Board on January 24, 2001, the Odeon Film Group has ceased to operate its Internet business. This resolution was announced in an ad-hoc release.

The film and TV entertainment portal Filmstadt.de has been closed in the first quarter of 2001. The e-commerce operations, which include the Janosch-shop, the Schloss-Einstein-shop have been sold to Bavaria Sonor Musikverlag und Merchandising GmbH, Gruenwald, by effect of April 01 respectively August 01, 2001. Only the sale of content with no corresponding expenses will be continued to an insignificant extent. Therefore the business segment Internet is no longer a discontinuing operation pursuant to IAS 35.8a as shown last year.

Segmental disclosures required by other standards

IAS 7

11.10 As mentioned in paragraph 9.5 IAS 7, 'Cash flow statements', encourages disclosure of the amount of cash flows arising from the operating, investing and financing activities of each reported business and geographical segment (see for example Table 12). [IAS 7 para 50(d)].

IAS 30

11.11 Paragraph 40 of IAS 30, 'Disclosures in the financial statements of banks and similar financial institutions', requires for banks and similar financial institutions disclosure of significant concentrations of risks. The disclosure requirements are that such entities should disclose any significant concentrations of its assets, liabilities and off balance sheet items. The disclosures should be made in terms of geographical areas, customer or industry group or other concentrations of risk. A bank should also disclose the amount of significant net foreign currency exposures. Such disclosures are made in addition to segment information required by IAS 14. [IAS 30 para 40]. IAS 30 paragraph 41 indicates that the disclosures are based on the analysis that is appropriate in the circumstances of the bank. For a bank, this IAS 30 analysis should be based on the geographical location of counterparties, whereas IAS 14 requires disclosure of segment assets based on the location of the entity entering into the transactions (for example, loans advanced to customers).

11.12 For example, for a bank located in Switzerland, assume that the business segments are the primary reporting format and the geographical segments are the secondary reporting format. Under IAS 14 the loans issued by the Switzerland office to customers in Russia should be included in segment assets of the geographical segment 'Switzerland'. However, interest revenue earned on these loans should be included in the geographical segment 'Russia'. This is because Switzerland is the country of origin of the loan and this is the basis for disclosure of assets, whereas Russia is the location of the customer, which is the basis for disclosure of revenue (see para 10.3). IAS 30 may then require information additional to that given under IAS 14. For example, if the Swiss bank has made significant loans to Russian customers it should disclose the amount of such loans by the geographical location 'Russia'.

IAS 34

11.13 IAS 34, 'Interim financial reporting', requires disclosure of segment revenue and segment result for business segments or geographical segments, whichever is the entity's primary reporting format. However, such disclosures are required in an entity's interim report only if that entity is required by IAS 14 to disclose segmental information in its annual financial statements. [IAS 34 para 16(g)].

IAS 35

11.14 IAS 35, 'Discontinuing operations', requires that disclosures relating to a discontinuing operation should identify the business or geographical segment in which the discontinuing operation is reported. In practice, such a discontinuing operation is often identified and reported separately. [IAS 35 para 27(b)]. Bayer, in its 2001 financial statements reports discontinuing operations as a separate segment (see Table 19).

Table 19 – Bayer AG - Annual Report – 31 December 2001

Notes on segment reporting (extract)
Business activities that Bayer has already divested or intends to divest are shown as **discontinuing operations**. These are the Haarmann & Reimer, Erdolchemie and Fibers business groups.

IAS 36

11.15 IAS 36, 'Impairment of assets', requires that where an entity applies IAS 14, it should disclose the following for each reportable segment based on the entity's primary reporting format:

■ The amount of impairment losses recognised in the income statement and directly in equity during the period.

■ The amount of reversals of impairment losses recognised in the income statement and directly in equity during the period.

[IAS 36 para 116].

11.16 IAS 36 requires that if an impairment loss on an individual asset is recognised or reversed in the period and is material to the financial statements of the entity as a whole, the entity should disclose the nature of the asset and reportable segment to which the asset belongs, based on the entity's primary reporting format. [IAS 36 para 117(c)].

11.17 If the material impairment or reversal of an impairment relates to a cash generating unit, the financial statements should give a description of the unit (such as whether it is a product line, a plant, a business operation, a geographical area, or a reportable segment as defined in IAS 14). It should also disclose the amount of the impairment loss recognised or reversed by class of assets and by reportable segment, based on the entity's primary reporting format as defined in IAS 14. [IAS 36 para 117(d)]. Ascom and Novartis are example of companies that have disclosed impairment charges separately in their 2001 and 2002 financial statements. MobilCom's 2001 charge is shown in Table 15.

Additional voluntary disclosures

11.18 In addition to the required disclosure under IAS 14, many entities provide additional voluntary segmental disclosures. Sometimes these are given in the management report rather than in the financial statements. Some of the types of additional disclosure and some (but not all) of the companies that have given the disclosure in their annual reports in 2002 are listed below:

■   Employees - Ascom, Wienerberger, Dyckerhoff, FLS Industries, Bayer.

■   Sales orders - ESEC, Ascom.

■   Research and development - Bayer, Novartis.

■   Environmental expenditure - Dyckerhoff.

■   EBITDA - Dyckerhoff, Wienerberger, Wella, Ascom, FLS Industries.

■   Taxation - Dairy Farm, FLS Industries.

Summary of disclosures

11.19 The table below sets out a summary of the disclosure requirements of the standard.

Primary format is business segments	Primary format is geographical segments by location of assets	Primary format is geographical segments by location of customers
Required primary disclosures:		
Revenue from external customers by business segment. [IAS 14 para 51].	Revenue from external customers by location of assets. [IAS 14 para 51].	Revenue from external customers by location of customers. [IAS 14 para 51].
Revenue from transactions with other segments by business segment. [IAS 14 para 51].	Revenue from transactions with other segments by location of assets. [IAS 14 para 51].	Revenue from transactions with other segments by location of customers. [IAS 14 para 51].

Primary format is business segments	Primary format is geographical segments by location of assets	Primary format is geographical segments by location of customers
Segment result by business segment. [IAS 14 para 52].	Segment result by location of assets. [IAS 14 para 52].	Segment result by location of customers. [IAS 14 para 52].
Carrying amount of segment assets by business segment. [IAS 14 para 55].	Carrying amount of segment assets by location of assets. [IAS 14 para 55].	Carrying amount of segment assets by location of customers. [IAS 14 para 55].
Segment liabilities by business segment. [IAS 14 para 56].	Segment liabilities by location of assets. [IAS 14 para 56].	Segment liabilities by location of customers. [IAS 14 para 56].
Cost in period to acquire property, plant, equipment, and intangibles by business segment. [IAS 14 para 57].	Cost in period to acquire property, plant, equipment, and intangibles by location of assets. [IAS 14 para 57].	Cost in period to acquire property, plant, equipment, and intangibles by location of customers. [IAS 14 para 57].
Depreciation and amortisation expense by business segment. [IAS 14 para 58].	Depreciation and amortisation expense by location of assets. [IAS 14 para 58].	Depreciation and amortisation expense by location of customers. [IAS 14 para 58].
Non-cash expenses other than depreciation and amortisation by business segment. [IAS 14 para 61].	Non-cash expenses other than depreciation and amortisation by location of assets. [IAS 14 para 61].	Non-cash expenses other than depreciation and amortisation by location of customers. [IAS 14 para 61].
Share of net profit or loss of [IAS 14 para 64] and investment in [IAS 14 para 66] equity method associates or joint ventures by business segment (if substantially all within a single business segment).	Share of net profit or loss of [IAS 14 para 64] and investment in [IAS 14 para 66] equity method associates or joint ventures by location of assets (if substantially all within a single segment).	Share of net profit or loss of [IAS 14 para 64] and investment in [IAS 14 para 66] equity method associates or joint ventures by location of customers (if substantially all within a single segment).

Primary format is business segments	**Primary format is geographical segments by location of assets**	**Primary format is geographical segments by location of customers**
Reconciliation of revenue, result, assets, and liabilities by business segment. [IAS 14 para 67].	Reconciliation of revenue, result, assets, and liabilities. [IAS 14 para 67].	Reconciliation of revenue, result, assets, and liabilities. [IAS 14 para 67].

Required secondary disclosures

Revenue from external customers by location of customers. [IAS 14 para 69].	Revenue from external customers by business segment. [IAS 14 para 70].	Revenue from external customers by business segment. [IAS 14 para 70].
Carrying amount of segment assets by location of assets. [IAS 14 para 69].	Carrying amount of segment assets by business segment. [IAS 14 para 70].	Carrying amount of segment assets by business segment. [IAS 14 para 70].
Cost in period to acquire property, plant, equipment, and intangibles by location of assets. [IAS 14 para 69].	Cost in period to acquire property, plant, equipment, and intangibles by business segment. [IAS 14 para 70].	Cost in period to acquire property, plant, equipment, and intangibles by business segment. [IAS 14 para 70].
	Revenue from external customers by geographical customers if different from location of assets. [IAS 14 para 71].	
		Carrying amount of segment assets by location of assets if different from location of customers. [IAS 14 para 72].
		Cost in period to acquire property, plant, equipment, and intangibles by location of assets if different from location of customers. [IAS 14 para 72].

Primary format is business segments	Primary format is geographical segments by location of assets	Primary format is geographical segments by location of customers
Other required disclosures:		
Revenue for any business or geographical segment whose external revenue is more than 10% of enterprise revenue, which is not a reportable segment because a majority of its revenue is from internal transfers. [IAS 14 para 74].	Revenue for any business or geographical segment whose external revenue is more than 10% of enterprise revenue, which is not a reportable segment because a majority of its revenue is from internal transfers. [IAS 14 para 74].	Revenue for any business or geographical segment whose external revenue is more than 10% of enterprise revenue, which is not a reportable segment because a majority of its revenue is from internal transfers. [IAS 14 para 74].
Basis of pricing inter-segment transfers and any change therein. [IAS 14 para 75].	Basis of pricing inter-segment transfers and any change therein. [IAS 14 para 75].	Basis of pricing inter-segment transfers and any change therein. [IAS 14 para 75].
Changes in segment accounting policies. [IAS 14 para 76].	Changes in segment accounting policies. [IAS 14 para 76].	Changes in segment accounting policies. [IAS 14 para 76].
Types of products and services in each business segment. [IAS 14 para 81].	Types of products and services in each business segment. [IAS 14 para 81].	Types of products and services in each business segment. [IAS 14 para 81].
Composition of each geographical segment. [IAS 14 para 81].	Composition of each geographical segment. [IAS 14 para 81].	Composition of each geographical segment. [IAS 14 para 81].

Chapter 12

First-time adoption of IFRS

12.1 In the UK all listed companies are required to apply EU-adopted international financial reporting standards in their consolidated financial statements for accounting periods beginning on or after 1 January 2005. The IASB's rules for first time adoption set out in IFRS 1, 'First-time adoption of international financial reporting standards', do not make any exception for IAS 14 to the general rule that comparative figures should be presented in accordance with IFRS 1. This means, for example, that a company that adopts IAS 14 in its financial statements for the year ending 31 December 2005 should present comparative information prepared under IAS 14 for the year ended 31 December 2004 in those financial statements.

Chapter 13

Companies Act 1985 requirements

13.1   The provisions of the Companies Act 1985 relating to segmental reporting, currently applicable to UK companies, are contained in Schedule 4 to the Act. However, it is likely that UK law will change so as to permit companies that are required to adopt IFRS to substitute the requirements in IFRS for most of the Act's Schedule 4 requirements. Therefore, the Act's rules may not apply to those companies required to adopt IFRS in 2005. In the meantime, the rules are summarised in the paragraphs below.

13.2   The Act's disclosure requirements in respect of segmental information are few in number. Except for the very limited exemptions granted to small companies by Schedule 8, all companies must comply with the Act's disclosure requirements, subject only to the specific exemptions allowed by it. Thus, unless they adopt the prejudicial override clause, as referred to in paragraph 13.7, or take advantage of the exemptions available to small companies referred to in paragraph 13.9 below, companies must include certain specified information in the notes to the profit and loss account, analysed by both class of business and geographical market.

13.3   Specifically, the Act requires that, where a company has carried on two or more classes of business during the financial year in question, and these, in the directors' opinion, differ substantially from each other, the notes to the financial statements must give:

- A description of each class of business.

- The amount of turnover that is attributable to each class of business.

[4 Sch 55(1)].

13.4 'Turnover' comprises the amounts a company derives from providing goods and services that fall within its ordinary activities, after deducting trade discounts, VAT and any other taxes based on the amounts it so derives. In this context, turnover will include that of both continuing and discontinued or discontinuing operations.

13.5 The definition of turnover also has implications for inter-segment sales, since it seems that these are to be included within the segmental analyses of turnover. In this event, it seems fundamental that the reader should be able to differentiate between third party sales and inter-segment sales, as the latter are eliminated on consolidation, on the grounds that they are unrealised at an aggregated reporting level.

13.6 Under the Act, where a company has supplied goods or services to two or more markets during the financial year in question, the turnover must also be disaggregated between markets. This is necessary, however, only if the directors believe that the markets differ substantially. For this purpose, 'market' means a market delineated by geographical bounds. [4 Sch 55(2)].

13.7 The Act states that, in determining the turnover attributable to each class of business, the directors must have regard to the way in which the company's activities are organised. [4 Sch 55(3)]. Where classes of business do not, in the directors' opinion, differ substantially, they are to be treated as one class. Similarly, where the directors believe that markets do not differ substantially, those markets are to be treated as one market. [4 Sch 55(4)]. In interpreting these matters the directors should have regard to the practical issues discussed from paragraph 4.2. They should also re-evaluate the position on each occasion that segmental information is published, to ensure that previous decisions on determining segments remain valid.

13.8 Segmental information need not be disclosed where the directors have determined that such disclosure would be seriously prejudicial to the company's interests. Where this exemption is utilised, however, the financial statements must state that disaggregated information has not been disclosed on the ground that disclosure would be prejudicial.

However, there is no requirement to give any further detail on why such disclosure would be prejudicial.

13.9   More recently, small companies (and groups headed by a small company) have been granted a specific exemption from the disclosure requirements of the Act. They need not give details of segmental information by market, as required by paragraph 55 of Schedule 4 to the Act, if they have taken advantage of the exemptions contained in Schedule 8 to the Act in drawing up their financial statements. However, if the company or group has supplied geographical markets outside the UK (turnover by destination), the notes must state the percentage of turnover (but not profit or loss) attributable to those markets. The analysis made for these purposes must still have regard to the manner in which the company's activities are organised. [8 Sch 49].

Chapter 14

Comparison of IAS 14 and UK GAAP

14.1 The corresponding UK accounting standard is SSAP 25, 'Segmental reporting'. A comparison of the rules in IAS 14 with UK GAAP is given in the table below.

IAS 14 and SSAP 25 — Segment reporting

IAS 14, Segment reporting	SSAP 25, Segmental reporting
Effective for accounting periods beginning on or after 1 July 1998.	*Effective for accounting periods beginning on or after 1 July 1990.*

Related pronouncements	
None.	None.

Overview

The scope of IAS 14 and SSAP 25 differs. IAS 14 applies to entities whose equity or debt securities are publicly traded or in the process of being so. SSAP 25 applies to public companies, banking and insurance companies and groups and certain other large entities. In addition, the UK Companies Act 1985 also contains certain segmental reporting requirements that apply to all companies.

The Act and SSAP 25 each contain an exemption from the disclosure requirements where disclosure would be seriously prejudicial to the entity's interests. There is no such exemption in IAS 14.

IAS 14 provides that one basis of segmentation is primary and the other is secondary, with considerably less information required to be disclosed for secondary segments. This differs from SSAP 25 which does not make such a distinction.

IAS 14 is based on management's approach to organising the business. An entity's internal organisational and management structure and its system of internal financial reporting to the board of directors and the chief executive officer should normally be the basis for determining which reporting format is primary and which is secondary. There are exceptions: if the entity's risks and rates of return are strongly affected by both products/services and geography; and if the internal reporting is not based on products/services or on geography. This management-based approach differs from the risk/returns approach of SSAP 25, although in practice the results may be similar.

The disclosure requirements of IAS 14 are more extensive than in SSAP 25.

Convergence

The IASB's project on reporting performance and the income statement may have implications for IAS 14. Also, the IASB has noted IAS 14 for review for convergence with US GAAP in due course.

IAS 14, Segment reporting	SSAP 25, Segment reporting

Summary of main points

Scope

Applies to public entities – those that have equity or debt securities that are publicly traded or those that are in the process of issuing equity or debt in public securities markets. [IAS 14 para 3].	Applies to public companies, banking and insurance companies/groups and large private companies. [SSAP 25 para 41].
Other entities are encouraged to voluntarily disclose segment information when complying with IAS. [IAS 14 paras 4, 5].	Similar. [SSAP 25 para 42].
If a subsidiary is a publicly traded entity it must comply with IAS 14 in its own financial report. [IAS 14 para 6].	Similar. Also a large private company, which is not a banking or insurance company, is exempt from SSAP 25 if its parent provides segmental information. [SSAP 25 para 41].
No seriously prejudicial exemption under IAS 14.	Seriously prejudicial exemption available. [SSAP 25 para 43].

Types of segments

Business segment is based on consideration of the following factors:

Similar. [SSAP 25 para 12].

• Nature of the products or services.

• Nature of the production processes.

• Type or class of customer for the products or services.

• Methods used to distribute the products or provide the services.

• If applicable, the nature of the regulatory environment, for example, banking, insurance, or public utilities.

[IAS 14 para 9].

Geographical segment is based on consideration of the following factors:

Similar to IAS 14, except that SSAP 25 states that although proximity of operations may indicate similar economic trends and risks this will not necessarily be the case. [SSAP 25 paras 15, 16].

• Similarity of economic and political conditions.

• Relationships between operations in different geographical areas.

• Proximity of operations.

• Special risks associated with operations in a particular area.

• Exchange control regulations.

• Underlying currency risks.

[IAS 14 para 9].

Geographical segments are based on either (a) the location of an entity's production or service facilities and other assets; or (b) the location of its markets and customers. [IAS 14 para 13].

Disclosures for turnover are required on both an 'origin' basis and a 'destination' basis (see below).

Identification of reportable segments

The dominant source and nature of an entity's risks and returns should govern whether its primary segment will be business segments or geographical segments. [IAS 14 para 26]. The basis for determining the primary segment should be derived from the entityâs risks and returns, its internal organisational and management structure and its system of internal financial reporting. [IAS 14 para 27].

Disclosure is based on classes of business and classes of geographical areas, with no distinction between a primary and secondary reporting segment. In identifying reportable segments management should have regard to the needs of the users of financial statements with respect to information on operations with differing returns on investment, degrees of risk, rates of growth and different potentials for future development. Note that there is no reference in SSAP 25 to internal financial reporting. [SSAP 25 para 8].

Reportable segments

A segment should be identified as reportable if a majority of its revenue is earned from sales to external customers and:

Similar to IAS 14, except that the requirement to contribute to ten per cent of 'total' revenue is based on third party revenue only and the assets test is replaced by ten per cent of 'net' assets. [SSAP 25 para 9].

• its revenue from sales to external customers (external revenue) and from transactions with other segments (internal revenue) is ten per cent or more of the total revenue, external and internal, of all segments; or

• its segment result, whether profit or loss, is ten per cent or more of the combined result of all segments in profit or the combined result of all segments in loss, whichever is the greater in absolute amount; or

• its assets are ten per cent or more of the total assets of all segments.

[IAS 14 para 35].

If less than 75 per cent of external revenue is attributable to reportable segments, additional segments should be identified – even if they do not meet the thresholds above. [IAS 14 para 37].	No equivalent requirement in SSAP 25.
IAS 14 encourages the voluntary reporting of vertically integrated activities as separate segments. [IAS 14 para 40].	No equivalent note in SSAP 25.

Accounting policies

Segment information should be prepared under accounting policies which are consistent with those of the financial statements of the entity. [IAS 14 para 44].	No specific mention in SSAP 25, but the same would apply.
Changes in accounting policies for segmental reporting that have a material effect on segmental information should be disclosed. The disclosure required includes:	Similar. [SSAP 25 para 39].

• Description of the nature of the change.

• Reasons for the change.

• The fact that comparative information has been restated or that it is impracticable to do so.

• The financial effect of the change, if it is reasonably determinable.

[IAS 14 para 76].

Disclosure

For the primary reporting format the following should be disclosed for each reportable segment:	For each business and geographical segment the following should be disclosed:

Segment revenue separating out sales to external customers and sales to other segments. [IAS 14 para 51].

Similar to IAS 14. Disclosure should be given based on turnover by origin and by destination (or a statement that turnover by destination is not materially different from turnover by origin). [SSAP 25 para 34].

Segment result. [IAS 14 para 52].

Similar to IAS 14. [SSAP 25 para 34].

Total carrying amount of segment assets. [IAS 14 para 55].

Not required by SSAP 25. An analysis of net assets is required to be disclosed. [SSAP 25 para 24].

Segment liabilities. [IAS 14 para 56].

Not required by SSAP 25.

Capital expenditure (on an accruals basis – not a cash basis). [IAS 14 para 57].

Not required by SSAP 25.

Depreciation and amortisation of segment assets included in segment result (not required if cash flow disclosures for segments, as encouraged by IAS 7, are given). [IAS 14 paras 58, 63].

Not required by SSAP 25.

Other significant non-cash expenses (not required if cash flow disclosures for segments, as encouraged by IAS 7, are given). [IAS 14 paras 61, 63].

Not required by SSAP 25.

For each reportable segment, the share of result and net assets of investments accounted for under the equity method, if substantially all of those equity accounted entities' operations are within that reportable segment. [IAS 14 paras 64 to 66].

Similar to IAS 14, except that SSAP 25 specifies that information is to be given for significant associated undertakings (20 per cent of total result or 20 per cent of total net assets). [SSAP 25 para 36].

Entities are encouraged (but not required) to disclose the nature and amount of exceptional items of segment revenue and expense. [IAS 14 para 59].

Not required per SSAP 25, but FRS 3 states that the effect of exceptional items on segment results should be disclosed where material. [FRS 3 para 53].

For secondary reporting segments, the segment revenue, total carrying amount of segment assets and capital expenditure should be disclosed. [IAS 14 paras 69 to 72].

Not applicable to SSAP 25.

A reconciliation to the figures in the financial statements should be provided. [IAS 14 para 67].

Similar to IAS 14. [SSAP 25 para 37].

If a segment is not reportable because it earns a majority of its revenue from sales to other segments, but if its revenue from sales to external customers is ten per cent or more of total entity external revenue, the entity should disclose that fact and the amounts of revenue from (a) sales to external customers and (b) internal sales to other segments. [IAS 14 para 74].

This would be a reportable segment under SSAP 25. [SSAP 25 para 9].

In measuring and reporting segment revenue from transactions with other segments, inter-segment transfers should be measured on the basis that the entity actually uses to price those transfers. Disclosure is required of the basis of pricing inter-segment transfers. [IAS 14 para 75].

No equivalent requirement in SSAP 25.

An indication of the types of products/ services in each reported business segment and the composition of geographical segments should be given. [IAS 14 para 81].

Similar to IAS 14. [SSAP 25 para 34].

Appendix

IAS 14 — Segment Reporting

This Standard is effective for financial statements covering periods beginning on or after 1 July 1998.

Paragraphs 116 and 117 of IAS 36, *Impairment of Assets*, set out certain disclosure requirements for reporting impairment losses by segment.

Introduction

This Standard ('IAS 14 (revised)') replaces IAS 14, *Reporting Financial Information by Segment* ('the original IAS 14'). IAS 14 (revised) is effective for accounting periods beginning on or after 1 July 1998. The major changes from the original IAS 14 are as follows.

1. The original IAS 14 applied to enterprises whose securities are publicly traded and other economically significant entities. IAS 14 (revised) applies to enterprises whose equity or debt securities are publicly traded, including enterprises in the process of issuing equity or debt securities in a public securities market, but not to other economically significant entities.

2. The original IAS 14 required that information be reported for industry segments and geographical segments. It provided only general guidance for identifying industry segments and geographical segments. It suggested that internal organisational groupings may provide a basis for determining reportable segments, or segment reporting may require reclassification of data. IAS 14 (revised) requires that information be reported for business segments and geographical segments. It provides more detailed guidance than the original IAS 14 for identifying business segments and geographical segments. It requires that an enterprise look to its internal organisational structure and internal reporting system for the purpose of identifying those segments. If internal segments are based neither on groups of related products and services nor on geography, IAS

14 (revised) requires that an enterprise should look to the next lower level of internal segmentation to identify its reportable segments.

3. The original IAS 14 required that the same quantity of information be reported for both industry segments and geographical segments. IAS 14 (revised) provides that one basis of segmentation is primary and the other is secondary, with considerably less information required to be disclosed for secondary segments.

4. The original IAS 14 was silent on whether segment information must be prepared using the accounting policies adopted for the consolidated or enterprise financial statements. IAS 14 (revised) requires that the same accounting policies be followed.

5. The original IAS 14 had allowed differences in the definition of segment result among enterprises. IAS 14 (revised) provides more detailed guidance than the original IAS 14 as to specific items of revenue and expense that should be included in or excluded from segment revenue and segment expense. Accordingly, IAS 14 (revised) provides for a standardised measure of segment result, but only to the extent that items of revenue and operating expense can be directly attributed or reasonably allocated to segments.

6. IAS 14 (revised) requires "symmetry" in the inclusion of items in segment result and in segment assets. If, for example, segment result reflects depreciation expense, the depreciable asset must be included in segment assets. The original IAS 14 was silent on this matter.

7. The original IAS 14 was silent on whether segments deemed too small for separate reporting could be combined with other segments or excluded from all reportable segments. IAS 14 (revised) provides that small internally reported segments that are not required to be separately reported may be combined with each other if they share a substantial number of the factors that define a business segment or geographical segment, or they may be combined with a similar significant segment for which information is reported internally if certain conditions are met.

8. The original IAS 14 was silent on whether geographical segments should be based on where the enterprise's assets are located (the origin of its sales) or on where its customers are located (the destination of its sales). IAS 14 (revised) requires that, whichever is the basis of an enterprise's geographical segments, several items of data must be presented on the other basis if significantly different.

9. The original IAS 14 required four principal items of information for both industry segments and geographical segments:

(a) sales or other operating revenues, distinguishing between revenue derived from customers outside the enterprise and revenue derived from other segments;

(b) segment result;

(c) segment assets employed; and

(d) the basis of inter-segment pricing.

For an enterprise's primary basis of segment reporting (business segments or geographical segments), IAS 14 (revised) requires those same four items of information plus:

(a) segment liabilities;

(b) cost of property, plant, equipment, and intangible assets acquired during the period;

(c) depreciation and amortisation expense;

(d) non-cash expenses other than depreciation and amortisation; and

(e) the enterprise's share of the net profit or loss of an associate, joint venture, or other investment accounted for under the equity method if substantially all of the associate's operations are within only that segment, and the amount of the related investment.

For an enterprise's secondary basis of segment reporting, IAS 14 (revised) drops the original IAS 14 requirement for segment result and replaces it with the cost of property, plant, equipment, and intangible assets acquired during the period.

10. The original IAS 14 was silent on whether prior period segment information presented for comparative purposes should be restated for a material change in segment accounting policies. IAS 14 (revised) requires restatement unless it is impracticable to do so.

11. IAS 14 (revised) requires that if total revenue from external customers for all reportable segments combined is less than 75 per cent of total enterprise revenue, then additional reportable segments should be identified until the 75 per cent level is reached.

12. The original IAS 14 allowed a different method of pricing inter-segment transfers to be used in segment data than was actually used to price the transfers. IAS 14 (revised) requires that inter-segment transfers be measured on the basis that the enterprise actually used to price the transfers.

13. IAS 14 (revised) requires disclosure of revenue for any segment not deemed reportable because it earns a majority of its revenue from sales to other segments if that segment's revenue from sales to external customers is 10 per cent or more of total enterprise revenue. The original IAS 14 had no comparable requirement.

Contents

International Accounting Standard IAS 14

Segment Reporting

Segment Reporting

International Accounting Standard 14 *Segment Reporting* (IAS 14) is set out in paragraphs 1-84 and Appendices A-C. All the paragraphs have equal authority but retain the IASC format of the Standard when it was adopted by the IASB. IAS 14 should be read in the context of its objective, the *Preface to International Financial Reporting Standards* and the *Framework for the Preparation and Presentation of Financial Statements*. These provide a basis for selecting and applying accounting policies in the absence of explicit guidance.

Objective

The objective of this Standard is to establish principles for reporting financial information by segment—information about the different types of products and services an enterprise produces and the different geographical areas in which it operates—to help users of financial statements:

(a)   better understand the enterprise's past performance;

(b)   better assess the enterprise's risks and returns; and

(c)   make more informed judgements about the enterprise as a whole.

Many enterprises provide groups of products and services or operate in geographical areas that are subject to differing rates of profitability, opportunities for growth, future prospects, and risks. Information about an enterprise's different types of products and services and its operations in different geographical areas — often called segment information — is relevant to assessing the risks and returns of a diversified or multinational enterprise but may not be determinable from the aggregated data. Therefore, segment information is widely regarded as necessary to meeting the needs of users of financial statements.

Scope

1. *This Standard should be applied in complete sets of published financial statements that comply with International Accounting Standards.*

2. A complete set of financial statements includes a balance sheet, income statement, cash flow statement, a statement showing changes in equity, and notes, as provided in IAS 1, *Presentation of Financial Statements.*

3. *This Standard should be applied by enterprises whose equity or debt securities are publicly traded and by enterprises that are in the process of issuing equity or debt securities in public securities markets.*

4. If an enterprise whose securities are not publicly traded prepares financial statements that comply with International Accounting Standards, that enterprise is encouraged to disclose financial information by segment voluntarily.

5. *If an enterprise whose securities are not publicly traded chooses to disclose segment information voluntarily in financial statements that comply with International Accounting Standards, that enterprise should comply fully with the requirements of this Standard.*

6. *If a single financial report contains both consolidated financial statements of an enterprise whose securities are publicly traded and the separate financial statements of the parent or one or more subsidiaries, segment information need be presented only on the basis of the consolidated financial statements. If a subsidiary is itself an enterprise whose securities are publicly traded, it will present segment information in its own separate financial report.*

7. *Similarly, if a single financial report contains both the financial statements of an enterprise whose securities are publicly traded and the separate financial statements of an equity method associate or joint venture in which the enterprise has a financial interest, segment information need be presented only on the basis of the enterprise's financial statements. If the equity method associate or joint venture is itself an enterprise whose securities are publicly traded, it will present segment information in its own separate financial report.*

Definitions

Definitions from Other International Accounting Standards

8. *The following terms are used in this Standard with the meanings specified in IAS 7, Cash Flow Statements; IAS 8, Net Profit or Loss for the period, Fundamental Errors and Changes in Accounting Policies; and IAS 18, Revenue:*

    <u>Operating activities</u> are the principal revenue-producing activities of an enterprise and other activities that are not investing or financing activities.

    <u>Accounting policies</u> are the specific principles, bases, conventions, rules and practices adopted by an enterprise in preparing and presenting financial statements.

    <u>Revenue</u> is the gross inflow of economic benefits during the period arising in the course of the ordinary activities of an enterprise when those inflows result in increases in equity, other than increases relating to contributions from equity participants.

Definitions of Business Segment and Geographical Segment

9. *The terms business segment and geographical segment are used in this Standard with the following meanings:*

A <u>business segment</u> is a distinguishable component of an enterprise that is engaged in providing an individual product or service or a group of related products or services and that is subject to risks and returns that are different from those of other business segments. Factors that should be considered in determining whether products and services are related include:

(a)   *the nature of the products or services;*

(b)   *the nature of the production processes;*

(c)   *the type or class of customer for the products or services;*

(d)   *the methods used to distribute the products or provide the services; and*

(e)   *if applicable, the nature of the regulatory environment, for example, banking, insurance, or public utilities.*

A <u>geographical segment</u> is a distinguishable component of an enterprise that is engaged in providing products or services within a particular economic environment and that is subject to risks and returns that are different from those of components operating in other economic environments. Factors that should be considered in identifying geographical segments include:

(a)   *similarity of economic and political conditions;*

(b)   *relationships between operations in different geographical areas;*

(c)   *proximity of operations;*

(d)   *special risks associated with operations in a particular area;*

(e)   *exchange control regulations; and*

(f)   the underlying currency risks.

A <u>reportable segment</u> is a business segment or a geographical segment identified based on the foregoing definitions for which segment information is required to be disclosed by this Standard.

10.   The factors in paragraph 9 for identifying business segments and geographical segments are not listed in any particular order.

11.   A single business segment does not include products and services with significantly differing risks and returns. While there may be dissimilarities with respect to one or several of the factors in the definition of a business segment, the products and services included in a single business segment are expected to be similar with respect to a majority of the factors.

12.   Similarly, a geographical segment does not include operations in economic environments with significantly differing risks and returns. A geographical segment may be a single country, a group of two or more countries, or a region within a country.

13.   The predominant sources of risks affect how most enterprises are organised and managed. Therefore, paragraph 27 of this Standard provides that an enterprise's organisational structure and its internal financial reporting system is the basis for identifying its segments. The risks and returns of an enterprise are influenced both by the geographical *location of its operations* (where its products are produced or where its service delivery activities are based) and also by the *location of its markets* (where its products are sold or services are rendered). The definition allows geographical segments to be based on either:

(a)   the location of an enterprise's production or service facilities and other assets; or

(b)   the location of its markets and customers.

14. An enterprise's organisational and internal reporting structure will normally provide evidence of whether its dominant source of geographical risks results from the location of its assets (the origin of its sales) or the location of its customers (the destination of its sales). Accordingly, an enterprise looks to this structure to determine whether its geographical segments should be based on the location of its assets or on the location of its customers.

15. Determining the composition of a business or geographical segment involves a certain amount of judgement. In making that judgement, enterprise management takes into account the objective of reporting financial information by segment as set forth in this Standard and the qualitative characteristics of financial statements as identified in the IASC *Framework for the Preparation and Presentation of Financial Statements*. Those qualitative characteristics include the relevance, reliability, and comparability over time of financial information that is reported about an enterprise's different groups of products and services and about its operations in particular geographical areas, and the usefulness of that information for assessing the risks and returns of the enterprise as a whole.

Definitions of Segment Revenue, Expense, Result, Assets, and Liabilities

16. *The following additional terms are used in this Standard with the meanings specified:*

   Segment revenue is revenue reported in the enterprise's income statement that is directly attributable to a segment and the relevant portion of enterprise revenue that can be allocated on a reasonable basis to a segment, whether from sales to external customers or from transactions with other segments of the same enterprise. Segment revenue does not include:

   (a) extraordinary items;

(b)   *interest or dividend income, including interest earned on advances or loans to other segments, unless the segment's operations are primarily of a financial nature; or*

(c)   *gains on sales of investments or gains on extinguishment of debt unless the segment's operations are primarily of a financial nature.*

Segment revenue includes an enterprise's share of profits or losses of associates, joint ventures, or other investments accounted for under the equity method only if those items are included in consolidated or total enterprise revenue.

Segment revenue includes a joint venturer's share of the revenue of a jointly controlled entity that is accounted for by proportionate consolidation in accordance with IAS 31, **Financial Reporting of Interests in Joint Ventures.**

<u>*Segment expense*</u> *is expense resulting from the operating activities of a segment that is directly attributable to the segment and the relevant portion of an expense that can be allocated on a reasonable basis to the segment, including expenses relating to sales to external customers and expenses relating to transactions with other segments of the same enterprise. Segment expense does not include:*

(a)   *extraordinary items;*

(b)   *interest, including interest incurred on advances or loans from other segments, unless the segment's operations are primarily of a financial nature;*

(c)   *losses on sales of investments or losses on extinguishment of debt unless the segment's operations are primarily of a financial nature;*

(d)   an enterprise's share of losses of associates, joint ventures, or other investments accounted for under the equity method;

(e)   income tax expense; or

(f)   general administrative expenses, head-office expenses, and other expenses that arise at the enterprise level and relate to the enterprise as a whole. However, costs are sometimes incurred at the enterprise level on behalf of a segment. Such costs are segment expenses if they relate to the segment's operating activities and they can be directly attributed or allocated to the segment on a reasonable basis.

Segment expense includes a joint venturer's share of the expenses of a jointly controlled entity that is accounted for by proportionate consolidation in accordance with IAS 31.

For a segment's operations that are primarily of a financial nature, interest income and interest expense may be reported as a single net amount for segment reporting purposes only if those items are netted in the consolidated or enterprise financial statements.

<u>Segment result</u> is segment revenue less segment expense. Segment result is determined before any adjustments for minority interest.

<u>Segment assets</u> are those operating assets that are employed by a segment in its operating activities and that either are directly attributable to the segment or can be allocated to the segment on a reasonable basis.

If a segment's segment result includes interest or dividend income, its segment assets include the related receivables, loans, investments, or other income-producing assets.

Segment assets do not include income tax assets.

Segment assets include investments accounted for under the equity method only if the profit or loss from such investments is included in segment revenue. Segment assets include a joint venturer's share of the operating assets of a jointly controlled entity that is accounted for by proportionate consolidation in accordance with IAS 31.

Segment assets are determined after deducting related allowances that are reported as direct offsets in the enterprise's balance sheet.

<u>Segment liabilities</u> are those operating liabilities that result from the operating activities of a segment and that either are directly attributable to the segment or can be allocated to the segment on a reasonable basis.

If a segment's segment result includes interest expense, its segment liabilities include the related interest-bearing liabilities.

Segment liabilities include a joint venturer's share of the liabilities of a jointly controlled entity that is accounted for by proportionate consolidation in accordance with IAS 31.

Segment liabilities do not include income tax liabilities.

<u>Segment accounting policies</u> are the accounting policies adopted for preparing and presenting the financial statements of the consolidated group or enterprise as well as those accounting policies that relate specifically to segment reporting.

17.   The definitions of segment revenue, segment expense, segment assets, and segment liabilities include amounts of such items that are directly attributable to a segment and amounts of such items that can be allocated to a segment on a reasonable basis. An enterprise looks to its internal financial reporting system as the

starting point for identifying those items that can be directly attributed, or reasonably allocated, to segments. That is, there is a presumption that amounts that have been identified with segments for internal financial reporting purposes are directly attributable or reasonably allocable to segments for the purpose of measuring the segment revenue, segment expense, segment assets, and segment liabilities of reportable segments.

18.   In some cases, however, a revenue, expense, asset, or liability may have been allocated to segments for internal financial reporting purposes on a basis that is understood by enterprise management but that could be deemed subjective, arbitrary, or difficult to understand by external users of financial statements. Such an allocation would not constitute a reasonable basis under the definitions of segment revenue, segment expense, segment assets, and segment liabilities in this Standard. Conversely, an enterprise may choose not to allocate some item of revenue, expense, asset, or liability for internal financial reporting purposes, even though a reasonable basis for doing so exists. Such an item is allocated pursuant to the definitions of segment revenue, segment expense, segment assets, and segment liabilities in this Standard.

19.   Examples of segment assets include current assets that are used in the operating activities of the segment, property, plant, and equipment, assets that are the subject of finance leases (IAS 17, Leases), and intangible assets. If a particular item of depreciation or amortisation is included in segment expense, the related asset is also included in segment assets. Segment assets do not include assets used for general enterprise or head-office purposes. Segment assets include operating assets shared by two or more segments if a reasonable basis for allocation exists. Segment assets include goodwill that is directly attributable to a segment or that can be allocated to a segment on a reasonable basis, and segment expense includes related amortisation of goodwill.

20.   Examples of segment liabilities include trade and other payables, accrued liabilities, customer advances, product warranty provi-

sions, and other claims relating to the provision of goods and services. Segment liabilities do not include borrowings, liabilities related to assets that are the subject of finance leases (IAS 17), and other liabilities that are incurred for financing rather than operating purposes. If interest expense is included in segment result, the related interest-bearing liability is included in segment liabilities. The liabilities of segments whose operations are not primarily of a financial nature do not include borrowings and similar liabilities because segment result represents an operating, rather than a net-of-financing, profit or loss. Further, because debt is often issued at the head-office level on an enterprise-wide basis, it is often not possible to directly attribute, or reasonably allocate, the interest-bearing liability to the segment.

21. Measurements of segment assets and liabilities include adjustments to the prior carrying amounts of the identifiable segment assets and segment liabilities of a company acquired in a business combination accounted for as a purchase, even if those adjustments are made only for the purpose of preparing consolidated financial statements and are not recorded in either the parent's or the subsidiary's separate financial statements. Similarly, if property, plant, and equipment has been revalued subsequent to acquisition in accordance with the alternative accounting treatment allowed by IAS 16, then measurements of segment assets reflect those revaluations.

22. Some guidance for cost allocation can be found in other International Accounting Standards. For example, paragraphs 8-16 of IAS 2, *Inventories*, provide guidance for attributing and allocating costs to inventories, and paragraphs 16-21 of IAS 11, Construction Contracts, provide guidance for attributing and allocating costs to contracts. That guidance may be useful in attributing or allocating costs to segments.

23. IAS 7, *Cash Flow Statements*, provides guidance as to whether bank overdrafts should be included as a component of cash or should be reported as borrowings.

24. Segment revenue, segment expense, segment assets, and segment liabilities are determined before intra-group balances and intra-group transactions are eliminated as part of the consolidation process, except to the extent that such intra-group balances and transactions are between group enterprises within a single segment.

25. While the accounting policies used in preparing and presenting the financial statements of the enterprise as a whole are also the fundamental segment accounting policies, segment accounting policies include, in addition, policies that relate specifically to segment reporting, such as identification of segments, method of pricing inter-segment transfers, and basis for allocating revenues and expenses to segments.

Identifying Reportable Segments

Primary and Secondary Segment Reporting Formats

26. The dominant source and nature of an enterprise's risks and returns should govern whether its primary segment reporting format will be business segments or geographical segments. If the enterprise's risks and rates of return are affected predominantly by differences in the products and services it produces, its primary format for reporting segment information should be business segments, with secondary information reported geographically. Similarly, if the enterprise's risks and rates of return are affected predominantly by the fact that it operates in different countries or other geographical areas, its primary format for reporting segment information should be geographical segments, with secondary information reported for groups of related products and services.

27. An enterprise's internal organisational and management structure and its system of internal financial reporting to the board of directors and the chief executive officer should normally be the basis for identifying the predominant source and nature of risks and differing rates of return facing the enterprise and, therefore, for determining which reporting format is primary and which is secondary, except as provided in subparagraphs (a) and (b) below:

(a)   if an enterprise's risks and rates of return are strongly affected both by differences in the products and services it produces and by differences in the geographical areas in which it operates, as evidenced by a "matrix approach" to managing the company and to reporting internally to the board of directors and the chief executive officer, then the enterprise should use business segments as its primary segment reporting format and geographical segments as its secondary reporting format; and

(b)   if an enterprise's internal organisational and management structure and its system of internal financial reporting to the board of directors and the chief executive officer are based neither on individual products or services or on groups of related products/ services nor on geography, the directors and management of the enterprise should determine whether the enterprise's risks and returns are related more to the products and services it produces or more to the geographical areas in which it operates and, as a consequence, should choose either business segments or geographical segments as the enterprise's primary segment reporting format, with the other as its secondary reporting format.

28.   For most enterprises, the predominant source of risks and returns determines how the enterprise is organised and managed. An enterprise's organisational and management structure and its internal financial reporting system normally provide the best

evidence of the enterprise's predominant source of risks and returns for purpose of its segment reporting. Therefore, except in rare circumstances, an enterprise will report segment information in its financial statements on the same basis as it reports internally to top management. Its predominant source of risks and returns becomes its primary segment reporting format. Its secondary source of risks and returns becomes its secondary segment reporting format.

29.   A "matrix presentation"—both business segments and geographical segments as primary segment reporting formats with full segment disclosures on each basis—often will provide useful information if an enterprise's risks and rates of return are strongly affected both by differences in the products and services it produces and by differences in the geographical areas in which it operates. This Standard does not require, but does not prohibit, a "matrix presentation".

30.   In some cases, an enterprise's organisation and internal reporting may have developed along lines unrelated either to differences in the types of products and services they produce or to the geographical areas in which they operate. For instance, internal reporting may be organised solely by legal entity, resulting in internal segments composed of groups of unrelated products and services. In those unusual cases, the internally reported segment data will not meet the objective of this Standard. Accordingly, paragraph 27(b) requires the directors and management of the enterprise to determine whether the enterprise's risks and returns are more product/service driven or geographically driven and to choose either business segments or geographical segments as the enterprise's primary basis of segment reporting. The objective is to achieve a reasonable degree of comparability with other enterprises, enhance understandability of the resulting information, and meet the expressed needs of investors, creditors, and others for information about product/service-related and geographically-related risks and returns.

Business and Geographical Segments

31.   An enterprise's business and geographical segments for external reporting purposes should be those organisational units for which information is reported to the board of directors and to the chief executive officer for the purpose of evaluating the unit's past performance and for making decisions about future allocations of resources, except as provided in paragraph 32.

32.   If an enterprise's internal organisational and management structure and its system of internal financial reporting to the board of directors and the chief executive officer are based neither on individual products or services or on groups of related products/services nor on geography, paragraph 27(b) requires that the directors and management of the enterprise should choose either business segments or geographical segments as the enterprise's primary segment reporting format based on their assessment of which reflects the primary source of the enterprise's risks and returns, with the other its secondary reporting format. In that case, the directors and management of the enterprise must determine its business segments and geographical segments for external reporting purposes based on the factors in the definitions in paragraph 9 of this Standard, rather than on the basis of its system of internal financial reporting to the board of directors and chief executive officer, consistent with the following:

(a)   if one or more of the segments reported internally to the directors and management is a business segment or a geographical segment based on the factors in the definitions in paragraph 9 but others are not, subparagraph (b) below should be applied only to those internal segments that do not meet the definitions in paragraph 9 (that is, an internally reported segment that meets the definition should not be further segmented);

(b)   *for those segments reported internally to the directors and management that do not satisfy the definitions in paragraph 9, management of the enterprise should look to the next lower level of internal segmentation that reports information along product and service lines or geographical lines, as appropriate under the definitions in paragraph 9 and;*

(c)   *if such an internally reported lower-level segment meets the definition of business segment or geographical segment based on the factors in paragraph 9, the criteria in paragraphs 34 and 35 for identifying reportable segments should be applied to that segment.*

33.   Under this Standard, most enterprises will identify their business and geographical segments as the organisational units for which information is reported to the board of directors (particularly the supervisory non-management directors, if any) and to the chief executive officer (the senior operating decision maker, which in some cases may be a group of several people) for the purpose of evaluating each unit's past performance and for making decisions about future allocations of resources. And even if an enterprise must apply paragraph 32 because its internal segments are not along product/service or geographical lines, it will look to the next lower level of internal segmentation that reports information along product and service lines or geographical lines rather than construct segments solely for external reporting purposes. This approach of looking to an enterprise's organisational and management structure and its internal financial reporting system to identify the enterprise's business and geographical segments for external reporting purposes is sometimes called the management approach, and the organisational components for which information is reported internally are sometimes called "operating segments".

Reportable Segments

34.   *Two or more internally reported business segments or geographical segments that are substantially similar may be combined as a single business segment or geographical segment. Two or more business segments or geographical segments are substantially similar only if:*

(a)   they exhibit similar long-term financial performance; and

(b)   they are similar in all of the factors in the appropriate definition in paragraph 9.

35.   *A business segment or geographical segment should be identified as a reportable segment if a majority of its revenue is earned from sales to external customers and:*

(a)   its revenue from sales to external customers and from transactions with other segments is 10 per cent or more of the total revenue, external and internal, of all segments; or

(b)   its segment result, whether profit or loss, is 10 per cent or more of the combined result of all segments in profit or the combined result of all segments in loss, whichever is the greater in absolute amount; or

(c)   its assets are 10 per cent or more of the total assets of all segments.

36.   *If an internally reported segment is below all of the thresholds of significance in paragraph 35:*

(a)   that segment may be designated as a reportable segment despite its size;

(b)   if not designated as a reportable segment despite its size, that segment may be combined into a separately reportable segment with one or more other similar internally reported segment(s) that are also below all of

>*the thresholds of significance in paragraph 35 (two or more business segments or geographical segments are similar if they share a majority of the factors in the appropriate definition in paragraph 9); and*

>*(c)   if that segment is not separately reported or combined, it should be included as an unallocated reconciling item.*

37.   If total external revenue attributable to reportable segments constitutes less than 75 per cent of the total consolidated or enterprise revenue, additional segments should be identified as reportable segments, even if they do not meet the 10 per cent thresholds in paragraph 35, until at least 75 per cent of total consolidated or enterprise revenue is included in reportable segments.

38.   The 10 per cent thresholds in this Standard are not intended to be a guide for determining materiality for any aspect of financial reporting other than identifying reportable business and geographical segments.

39.   By limiting reportable segments to those that earn a majority of their revenue from sales to external customers, this Standard does not require that the different stages of vertically integrated operations be identified as separate business segments. However, in some industries, current practice is to report certain vertically integrated activities as separate business segments even if they do not generate significant external sales revenue. For instance, many international oil companies report their upstream activities (exploration and production) and their downstream activities (refining and marketing) as separate business segments even if most or all of the upstream product (crude petroleum) is transferred internally to the enterprise's refining operation.

40.   This Standard encourages, but does not require, the voluntary reporting of vertically integrated activities as separate segments,

with appropriate description including disclosure of the basis of pricing inter-segment transfers as required by paragraph 75.

41.   *If an enterprise's internal reporting system treats vertically integrated activities as separate segments and the enterprise does not choose to report them externally as business segments, the selling segment should be combined into the buying segment(s) in identifying externally reportable business segments unless there is no reasonable basis for doing so, in which case the selling segment would be included as an unallocated reconciling item.*

42.   *A segment identified as a reportable segment in the immediately preceding period because it satisfied the relevant 10 per cent thresholds should continue to be a reportable segment for the current period notwithstanding that its revenue, result, and assets all no longer exceed the 10 per cent thresholds, if the management of the enterprise judges the segment to be of continuing significance.*

43.   *If a segment is identified as a reportable segment in the current period because it satisfies the relevant 10 per cent thresholds, prior period segment data that is presented for comparative purposes should be restated to reflect the newly reportable segment as a separate segment, even if that segment did not satisfy the 10 per cent thresholds in the prior period, unless it is impracticable to do so.*

Segment Accounting Policies

44.   *Segment information should be prepared in conformity with the accounting policies adopted for preparing and presenting the financial statements of the consolidated group or enterprise.*

45.   There is a presumption that the accounting policies that the directors and management of an enterprise have chosen to use, in preparing its consolidated or enterprise-wide financial statements,

are those that the directors and management believe are the most appropriate for external reporting purposes. Since the purpose of segment information is to help users of financial statements better understand and make more informed judgements about the enterprise as a whole, this Standard requires the use, in preparing segment information, of the accounting policies that the directors and management have chosen. That does not mean, however, that the consolidated or enterprise accounting policies are to be applied to reportable segments as if the segments were separate stand-alone reporting entities. A detailed calculation done in applying a particular accounting policy at the enterprise-wide level may be allocated to segments if there is a reasonable basis for doing so. Pension calculations, for example, often are done for an enterprise as a whole, but the enterprise-wide figures may be allocated to segments based on salary and demographic data for the segments.

46. This Standard does not prohibit the disclosure of additional segment information that is prepared on a basis other than the accounting policies adopted for the consolidated or enterprise financial statements provided that (a) the information is reported internally to the board of directors and the chief executive officer for purposes of making decisions about allocating resources to the segment and assessing its performance and (b) the basis of measurement for this additional information is clearly described.

47. *Assets that are jointly used by two or more segments should be allocated to segments if, and only if, their related revenues and expenses also are allocated to those segments.*

48. The way in which asset, liability, revenue, and expense items are allocated to segments depends on such factors as the nature of those items, the activities conducted by the segment, and the relative autonomy of that segment. It is not possible or appropriate to specify a single basis of allocation that should be adopted by all enterprises. Nor is it appropriate to force allocation of enterprise

asset, liability, revenue, and expense items that relate jointly to two or more segments, if the only basis for making those allocations is arbitrary or difficult to understand. At the same time, the definitions of segment revenue, segment expense, segment assets, and segment liabilities are interrelated, and the resulting allocations should be consistent. Therefore, jointly used assets are allocated to segments if, and only if, their related revenues and expenses also are allocated to those segments. For example, an asset is included in segment assets if, and only if, the related depreciation or amortisation is deducted in measuring segment result.

Disclosure

49.   Paragraphs 50-67 specify the disclosures required for reportable segments for an enterprise's *primary* segment reporting format. Paragraphs 68-72 identify the disclosures required for an enterprise's *secondary* reporting format. Enterprises are encouraged to present all of the primary-segment disclosures identified in paragraphs 50-67 for each reportable secondary segment, although paragraphs 68-72 require considerably less disclosure on the secondary basis. Paragraphs 74-83 address several other segment disclosure matters. Appendix B to this Standard illustrates application of these disclosure standards.

Primary Reporting Format

50.   The disclosure requirements in paragraphs 51-67 should be applied to each reportable segment based on an enterprise's primary reporting format.

51.   An enterprise should disclose segment revenue for each reportable segment. Segment revenue from sales to external customers and segment revenue from transactions with other segments should be separately reported.

52. *An enterprise should disclose segment result for each reportable segment.*

53. If an enterprise can compute segment net profit or loss or some other measure of segment profitability other than segment result without arbitrary allocations, reporting of such amount(s) is encouraged in addition to segment result, appropriately described. If that measure is prepared on a basis other than the accounting policies adopted for the consolidated or enterprise financial statements, the enterprise will include in its financial statements a clear description of the basis of measurement.

54. An example of a measure of segment performance above segment result on the income statement is gross margin on sales. Examples of measures of segment performance below segment result on the income statement are profit or loss from ordinary activities (either before or after income taxes) and net profit or loss.

55. *An enterprise should disclose the total carrying amount of segment assets for each reportable segment.*

56. *An enterprise should disclose segment liabilities for each reportable segment.*

57. *An enterprise should disclose the total cost incurred during the period to acquire segment assets that are expected to be used during more than one period (property, plant, equipment, and intangible assets) for each reportable segment. While this sometimes is referred to as capital additions or capital expenditure, the measurement required by this principle should be on an accrual basis, not a cash basis.*

58. *An enterprise should disclose the total amount of expense included in segment result for depreciation and amortisation of segment assets for the period for each reportable segment.*

59. *An enterprise is encouraged, but not required to disclose the nature and amount of any items of segment revenue and segment expense that are of such size, nature, or incidence that their disclosure is relevant to explain the performance of each reportable segment for the period.*

60.   IAS 8 requires that when items of income or expense within profit or loss from ordinary activities are of such size, nature, or incidence that their disclosure is relevant to explain the performance of the enterprise for the period, the nature and amount of such items should be disclosed separately. IAS 8 offers a number of examples, including write-downs of inventories and property, plant, and equipment, provisions for restructurings, disposals of property, plant, and equipment and long-term investments, discontinued operations, litigation settlements, and reversals of provisions. Paragraph 59 is not intended to change the classification of any such items of revenue or expense from ordinary to extraordinary (as defined in IAS 8) or to change the measurement of such items. The disclosure encouraged by that paragraph, however, does change the level at which the significance of such items is evaluated for disclosure purposes from the enterprise level to the segment level.

61. *An enterprise should disclose, for each reportable segment, the total amount of significant non-cash expenses, other than depreciation and amortisation for which separate disclosure is required by paragraph 58, that were included in segment expense and, therefore, deducted in measuring segment result.*

62.   IAS 7 requires that an enterprise present a cash flow statement that separately reports cash flows from operating, investing, and financing activities. IAS 7 notes that disclosing cash flow information for each reportable industry and geographical segment is relevant to understanding the enterprise's overall financial position, liquidity, and cash flows. IAS 7 encourages the disclosure of such information. This Standard also encourages the

segment cash flow disclosures that are encouraged by IAS 7. Additionally, it encourages disclosure of significant non-cash revenues that were included in segment revenue and, therefore, added in measuring segment result.

63. *An enterprise that provides the segment cash flow disclosures that are encouraged by IAS 7 need not also disclose depreciation and amortisation expense pursuant to paragraph 58 or non-cash expenses pursuant to paragraph 61.*

64. *An enterprise should disclose, for each reportable segment, the aggregate of the enterprise's share of the net profit or loss of associates, joint ventures, or other investments accounted for under the equity method if substantially all of those associates' operations are within that single segment.*

65. While a single aggregate amount is disclosed pursuant to the preceding paragraph, each associate, joint venture, or other equity method investment is assessed individually to determine whether its operations are substantially all within a segment.

66. *If an enterprise's aggregate share of the net profit or loss of associates, joint ventures, or other investments accounted for under the equity method is disclosed by reportable segment, the aggregate investments in those associates and joint ventures should also be disclosed by reportable segment.*

67. *An enterprise should present a reconciliation between the information disclosed for reportable segments and the aggre-gated information in the consolidated or enterprise financial statements. In presenting the reconciliation, segment revenue should be reconciled to enterprise revenue from external customers (including disclosure of the amount of enterprise revenue from external customers not included in any segment's revenue); segment result should be reconciled to a comparable measure of enterprise operating profit or loss as well as to enterprise net profit or loss; segment assets should be reconciled*

to enterprise assets; and segment liabilities should be reconciled to enterprise liabilities.

Secondary Segment Information

68.   Paragraphs 50-67 identify the disclosure requirements to be applied to each reportable segment based on an enterprise's primary reporting format. Paragraphs 69-72 identify the disclosure requirements to be applied to each reportable segment based on an enterprise's secondary reporting format, as follows:

   (a)   if an enterprise's primary format is business segments, the required secondary-format disclosures are identified in paragraph 69;

   (b)   if an enterprise's primary format is geographical segments based on location of assets (where the enterprise's products are produced or where its service delivery operations are based), the required secondary-format disclosures are identified in paragraphs 70 and 71;

   (c)   if an enterprise's primary format is geographical segments based on the location of its customers (where its products are sold or services are rendered), the required secondary-format disclosures are identified in paragraphs 70 and 72.

69.   *If an enterprise's primary format for reporting segment information is business segments, it should also report the following information:*

   (a)   segment revenue from external customers by geographical area based on the geographical location of its customers, for each geographical segment whose revenue from sales to external customers is 10 per cent or more of total enterprise revenue from sales to all external customers;

(b)   the total carrying amount of segment assets by geographical location of assets, for each geographical segment whose segment assets are 10 per cent or more of the total assets of all geographical segments; and

(c)   the total cost incurred during the period to acquire segment assets that are expected to be used during more than one period (property, plant, equipment, and intangible assets) by geographical location of assets, for each geographical segment whose segment assets are 10 per cent or more of the total assets of all geographical segments.

70.   If an enterprise's primary format for reporting segment information is geographical segments (whether based on location of assets or location of customers), it should also report the following segment information for each business segment whose revenue from sales to external customers is 10 per cent or more of total enterprise revenue from sales to all external customers or whose segment assets are 10 per cent or more of the total assets of all business segments:

(a)   segment revenue from external customers;

(b)   the total carrying amount of segment assets; and

(c)   the total cost incurred during the period to acquire segment assets that are expected to be used during more than one period (property, plant, equipment, and intangible assets).

71.   If an enterprise's primary format for reporting segment information is geographical segments that are based on location of assets, and if the location of its customers is different from the location of its assets, then the enterprise should also report revenue from sales to external customers for each customer-based geographical segment whose revenue from sales to

external customers is 10 per cent or more of total enterprise revenue from sales to all external customers.

72.   *If an enterprise's primary format for reporting segment information is geographical segments that are based on location of customers, and if the enterprise's assets are located in different geographical areas from its customers, then the enterprise should also report the following segment information for each asset-based geographical segment whose revenue from sales to external customers or segment assets are 10 per cent or more of related consolidated or total enterprise amounts:*

(a)   *the total carrying amount of segment assets by geographical location of the assets; and*

(b)   *the total cost incurred during the period to acquire segment assets that are expected to be used during more than one period (property, plant, equipment, and intangible assets) by location of the assets.*

Illustrative Segment Disclosures

73.   Appendix B to this Standard presents an illustration of the disclosures for primary and secondary reporting formats that are required by this Standard.

Other Disclosure Matters

74.   *If a business segment or geographical segment for which information is reported to the board of directors and chief executive officer is not a reportable segment because it earns a majority of its revenue from sales to other segments, but nonetheless its revenue from sales to external customers is 10 per cent or more of total enterprise revenue from sales to all external customers, the enterprise should disclose that fact and the amounts of revenue from (a) sales to external customers and (b) internal sales to other segments.*

75.	*In measuring and reporting segment revenue from transactions with other segments, inter-segment transfers should be measured on the basis that the enterprise actually used to price those transfers. The basis of pricing inter-segment transfers and any change therein should be disclosed in the financial statements.*

76.	*Changes in accounting policies adopted for segment reporting that have a material effect on segment information should be disclosed, and prior period segment information presented for comparative purposes should be restated unless it is impracticable to do so. Such disclosure should include a description of the nature of the change, the reasons for the change, the fact that comparative information has been restated or that it is impracticable to do so, and the financial effect of the change, if it is reasonably determinable. If an enterprise changes the identification of its segments and it does not restate prior period segment information on the new basis because it is impracticable to do so, then for the purpose of comparison the enterprise should report segment data for both the old and the new bases of segmentation in the year in which it changes the identification of its segments.*

77.	Changes in accounting policies adopted by the enterprise are dealt with in IAS 8. IAS 8 requires that changes in accounting policy should be made only if required by statute, or by an accounting standard-setting body, or if the change will result in a more appropriate presentation of events or transactions in the financial statements of the enterprise.

78.	Changes in accounting policies adopted at the enterprise level that affect segment information are dealt with in accordance with IAS 8. Unless a new International Accounting Standard specifies otherwise, IAS 8 requires that a change in accounting policy should be applied retrospectively and that prior period information be restated unless it is impracticable to do so (benchmark treatment) or that the cumulative adjustment resulting from the change be included in determining the enterprise's net profit or loss for the current period (allowed alternative treatment). If the benchmark treatment is followed, prior period segment information will be restated. If the allowed alternative is followed, the cumulative adjustment that is included in determining the enterprise's net profit or loss is included in segment result if it is an operating item that can be attributed or reasonably allocated to segments. In the latter case, IAS 8 may require separate disclosure if its size, nature, or incidence is such that the disclosure is relevant to explain the performance of the enterprise for the period.

79.   Some changes in accounting policies relate specifically to segment reporting. Examples include changes in identification of segments and changes in the basis for allocating revenues and expenses to segments. Such changes can have a significant impact on the segment information reported but will not change aggregate financial information reported for the enterprise. To enable users to understand the changes and to assess trends, prior period segment information that is included in the financial statements for comparative purposes is restated, if practicable, to reflect the new accounting policy.

80.   Paragraph 75 requires that, for segment reporting purposes, inter-segment transfers should be measured on the basis that the enterprise actually used to price those transfers. If an enterprise changes the method that it actually uses to price inter-segment transfers, that is not a change in accounting policy for which prior period segment data should be restated pursuant to paragraph 76. However, paragraph 75 requires disclosure of the change.

81.   An enterprise should indicate the types of products and services included in each reported business segment and indicate the composition of each reported geographical segment, both primary and secondary, if not otherwise disclosed in the financial statements or elsewhere in the financial report.

82. To assess the impact of such matters as shifts in demand, changes in the price of inputs or other factors of production, and the development of alternative products and processes on a business segment, it is necessary to know the activities encompassed by that segment. Similarly, to assess the impact of changes in the economic and political environment on the risks and rates of returns of a geographical segment, it is important to know the composition of that geographical segment.

83. Previously reported segments that no longer satisfy the quantitative thresholds are not reported separately. They may no longer satisfy those thresholds, for example, because of a decline in demand or a change in management strategy or because a part of the operations of the segment has been sold or combined with other segments. An explanation of the reasons why a previously reported segment is no longer reported may also be useful in confirming expectations regarding declining markets and changes in enterprise strategies.

Effective Date

84. *This International Accounting Standard becomes operative for financial statements covering periods beginning on or after 1 July 1998. Earlier application is encouraged. If an enterprise applies this Standard for financial statements covering periods beginning before 1 July 1998 instead of the original IAS 14, the enterprise should disclose that fact. If financial statements include comparative information for periods prior to the effective date or earlier voluntary adoption of this Standard, restatement of segment data included therein to conform to the provisions of this Standard is required unless it is not practicable to do so, in which case the enterprise should disclose that fact.*

Appendix A

Segment Definition Decision Tree

The purpose of this appendix is to illustrate the application of paragraphs 31–43.

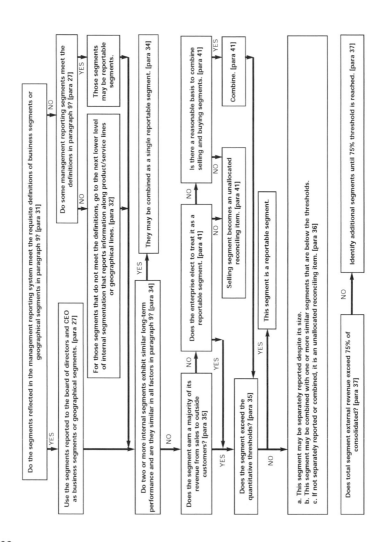

Appendix B

Illustrative Segment Disclosures

The appendix is illustrative only and does not form part of the Standard. The purpose of the appendix is to illustrate the application of the Standard to assist in clarifying its meaning.

The schedule and related note presented in this Appendix illustrate the segment disclosures that this Standard would require for a diversified multinational business enterprise. This example is intentionally complex to illustrate most of the provisions of this Standard. For illustrative purposes, the example presents comparative data for two years. Segment data is required for each year for which a complete set of financial statements is presented.

SCHEDULE A - INFORMATION ABOUT BUSINESS SEGMENTS (Note 4)

(All amounts million)

	Paper Products		Office Products		Publishing		Other Operations		Eliminations		Consolidated	
	20x2	20x1	20x2	20x1	20x2	20x1	20x2	20x1	20x2	20x1	20x2	20x1
REVENUE												
External sales	55	50	20	17	19	16	7	7				
Inter-segment sales	15	10	10	14	2	4	2	2	(29)	(30)		
Total revenue	70	60	30	31	21	20	9	9	(29)	(30)	101	90
RESULT												
Segment result	20	17	9	7	2	1	0	0	(1)	(1)	30	24
Unallocated corporate expenses											(7)	(9)
Operating profit											23	15
Interest expense											(4)	(4)
Interest income											2	3
Share of net profits of associates	6	5					2	2			8	7
Income taxes											(7)	(4)
Profit from ordinary activities											22	17
Extraordinary loss: uninsured earthquake damage to factory		(3)										(3)
Net profit											22	14

OTHER INFORMATION	Paper Products 20x2	20x1	Office Products 20x2	20x1	Publishing 20x2	20x1	Other Operations 20x2	20x1	Eliminations 20x2	20x1	Consolidated 20x2	20x1
Segment assets	54	50	34	30	10	10	10	9			108	99
Investment in equity method associates	20	16					12	10			32	26
Unallocated corporate assets											35	30
Consolidated total assets											175	155
Segment liabilities	25	15	8	11	8	8	1	1			42	35
Unallocated corporate liabilities											40	55
Consolidated total liabilities											82	90
Capital expenditure	12	10	3	5	5		4	3				
Depreciation	9	7	9	7	5	3	3	4				
Non-cash expenses other than depreciation	8	2	7	3	2	2	2	1				

Note 4—Business and Geographical Segments (all amounts million)

Business segments: for management purposes, the Company is organised on a worldwide basis into three major operating divisions—paper products, office products and publishing—each Head Ed by a senior vice president. The divisions are the basis on which the Company reports its primary segment information. The paper products segment produces a broad range of writing and publishing papers and newsprint. The office products segment manufactures labels, binders, pens, and markers and also distributes office products made by others. The publishing segment develops and sells loose-leaf services, bound volumes and CD-ROM products in the fields of taxation, law and accounting. Other operations include development of computer software for specialised business applications for unaffiliated customers and development of certain former productive timberlands into vacation home sites. Financial information about business segments is presented in schedule A.

Geographical segments: although the Company's three divisions are managed on a worldwide basis, they operate in four principal geographical areas of the world. In the United Kingdom, its home country, the Company produces and sells a broad range of papers and office products. Additionally, all of the Company's publishing and computer software development operations are conducted in the United Kingdom, though the published loose-leaf and bound volumes and CD-ROM products are sold throughout the United Kingdom and Western Europe. In the European Union, the Company operates paper and office products manufacturing facilities and sales offices in the following countries: France, Belgium, Germany and the Netherlands. Operations in Canada and the United States are essentially similar and consist of manufacturing papers and newsprint that are sold entirely within those two countries. Most of the paper pulp comes from Company-owned timberlands in the two countries. Operations in Indonesia include the production of paper pulp and the manufacture of writing and publishing papers and office products, almost all of which is sold outside Indonesia, both to other segments of the Company and to external customers.

Sales by market: the following table shows the distribution of the Company's consolidated sales by geographical market, regardless of where the goods were produced:

	Sales Revenue by Geographical Market	
	20x2	**20x1**
United Kingdom	19	22
Other European Union countries	30	31
Canada and the United States	28	21
Mexico and South America	6	2
Southeast Asia (principally Japan and Taiwan)	<u>18</u>	<u>14</u>
	<u>101</u>	<u>90</u>

Assets and additions to property, plant, equipment, and intangible assets by geographical area: the following tables show the carrying amount of segment assets and additions to property, plant, equipment, and intangible assets by geographical area in which the assets are located:

	Carrying Amount of Segment Assets	Additions to Property, Plant, Equipment, and Intangible Assets		
	20x2	20x1	20x2	20x1
United Kingdom	72	78	8	5
Other European Union countries	47	37	5	4
Canada and the United States	34	20	4	3
Indonesia	22	20	7	6
	175	155	24	18

Segment revenue and expense: in Belgium, paper and office products are manufactured in combined facilities and are sold by a combined sales force. Joint revenues and expenses are allocated to the two business segments. All other segment revenue and expense is directly attributable to the segments.

Segment assets and liabilities: segment assets include all operating assets used by a segment and consist principally of operating cash, receivables, inventories and property, plant and equipment, net of allowances and provisions. While most such assets can be directly attributed to individual segments, the carrying amount of certain assets used jointly by two or more segments is allocated to the segments on a reasonable basis. Segment liabilities include all operating liabilities and consist principally of accounts, wages, and taxes currently payable and accrued liabilities. Segment assets and liabilities do not include deferred income taxes.

Inter-segment transfers: segment revenue, segment expenses and segment result include transfers between business segments and between geographical segments. Such transfers are accounted for at competitive market prices charged to unaffiliated customers for similar goods. Those transfers are eliminated in consolidation.

Unusual item: sales of office products to external customers in 20x2 were adversely affected by a lengthy strike of transportation workers in the United Kingdom, which interrupted product shipments for approximately four months. The Company estimates that sales of office products were approximately half of what they would otherwise have been during the four-month period.

Investment in equity method associates: the Company owns 40 per cent of the capital stock of EuroPaper, Ltd., a specialist paper manufacturer with operations principally in Spain and the United Kingdom. The investment is accounted for by the equity method. Although the investment and the Company's share of EuroPaper's net profit are excluded from segment assets and segment revenue, they are shown separately in conjunction with data for the paper products segment. The Company also owns several small equity method investments in Canada and the United States whose operations are dissimilar to any of the three business segments.

Extraordinary loss: as more fully discussed in Note 6, the Company incurred an uninsured loss of 3 million caused by earthquake damage to a paper mill in Belgium in November 20x1.

Appendix C

Summary of Required Disclosure

The appendix is illustrative only and does not form part of the Standard. Its purpose is to summarise the disclosures required by paragraphs 49-83 for each of the three possible primary segment reporting formats.

[¶xx] refers to paragraph xx in the Standard.

PRIMARY FORMAT IS BUSINESS SEGMENTS	PRIMARY FORMAT IS GEOGRAPHICAL SEGMENTS BY LOCATION OF ASSETS	PRIMARY FORMAT IS GEOGRAPHICAL SEGMENTS BY LOCATION OF CUSTOMERS
Required Primary Disclosures:	*Required Primary Disclosures:*	*Required Primary Disclosures:*
Revenue from external customers by business segment [¶51]	Revenue from external customers by location of assets [¶51]	Revenue from external customers by location of customers [¶51]
Revenue from transactions with other segments by business segment [¶51]	Revenue from transactions with other segments by location of assets [¶51]	Revenue from transactions with other segments by location of customers [¶51]
Segment result by business segment [¶52]	Segment result by location of assets [¶52]	Segment result by location of customers [¶52]
Carrying amount of segment assets by business segment [¶55]	Carrying amount of segment assets by location of assets [¶55]	Carrying amount of segment assets by location of customers [¶55]
Segment liabilities by business segment [¶56]	Segment liabilities by location of assets [¶56]	Segment liabilities by location of customers [¶56]
Cost to acquire property, plant, equipment, and intangibles by business segment [¶57]	Cost to acquire property, plant, equipment, and intangibles by location of assets [¶57]	Cost to acquire property, plant, equipment, and intangibles by location of customers [¶57]
Depreciation and amortisation expense by business segment [¶58]	Depreciation and amortisation expense by location of assets [¶58]	Depreciation and amortisation expense by location of customers [¶58]

128

Non-cash expenses other than depreciation and amortisation by business segment [¶61]	Non-cash expenses other than depreciation and amortisation by location of assets [¶61]	Non-cash expenses other than depreciation and amortisation by location of customers [¶61]
Share of net profit or loss of [¶64] and investment in [¶66] equity method associates or joint ventures by business segment (if substantially all within a single business segment)	Share of net profit or loss of [¶64] and investment in [¶66] equity method associates or joint ventures by location of assets (if substantially all within a single segment)	Share of net profit or loss of [¶64] and investment in [¶66] equity method associates or joint ventures by location of customers (if substantially all within a single segment)
Reconciliation of revenue, result, assets, and liabilities by business segment [¶67]	Reconciliation of revenue, result, assets, and liabilities [¶67]	Reconciliation of revenue, result, assets, and liabilities [¶67]
Revenue from external customers by location of customers [¶69]	Revenue from external customers by business segment [¶70]	Revenue from external customers by business segment [¶70]
Carrying amount of segment assets by location of assets [¶69]	Carrying amount of segment assets by business segment [¶70]	Carrying amount of segment assets by business segment [¶70]
Cost to acquire property, plant, equipment, and intangibles by location of assets [¶69]	Cost to acquire property, plant, equipment, and intangibles by business segment [¶70]	Cost to acquire property, plant, equipment, and intangibles by business segment [¶70]
	Revenue from external customers by geographical customers if different from location of assets [¶71]	
		Carrying amount of segment assets by location of assets if different from location of customers [¶72]
		Cost to acquire property, plant, equipment, and intangibles by location of assets if different from location of customers [¶72]

Revenue for any business or geographical segment whose external revenue is more than 10 per cent of enterprise revenue but that is not a reportable segment because a majority of its revenue is from internal transfers [¶74]	Revenue for any business or geographical segment whose external revenue is more than 10 per cent of enterprise revenue but that is not a reportable segment because a majority of its revenue is from internal transfers [¶74]	Revenue for any business or geographical segment whose external revenue is more than 10 per cent of enterprise revenue but that is not a reportable segment because a majority of its revenue is from internal transfers [¶74]
Basis of pricing inter-segment transfers and any change therein [¶75]	Basis of pricing inter-segment transfers and any change therein [¶75]	Basis of pricing inter-segment transfers and any change therein [¶75]
Changes in segment accounting policies [¶76]	Changes in segment accounting policies [¶76]	Changes in segment accounting policies [¶76]
Types of products and services in each business segment [¶81]	Types of products and services in each business segment [¶81]	Types of products and services in each business segment [¶81]
Composition of each geographical segment [¶81]	Composition of each geographical segment [¶81]	Composition of each geographical segment [¶81]